THE SKY IS FALLING, THE CHURCH IS DYING

AND OTHER FALSE ALARMS

Other Abingdon Press Books by Ted A. Campbell

Methodist Doctrine: The Essentials

Wesley and the Quadrilateral: Renewing the Conversation

Wesleyan Beliefs: Formal and Popular Expressions of the Core Beliefs of Wesleyan Communities

Wesleyan Essentials in a Multicultural Society, with Michael T. Burns

THE SKY IS FALLING, THE CHURCH IS DYING

AND OTHER FALSE ALARMS

Ted A. Campbell

Nashville

THE SKY IS FALLING, THE CHURCH IS DYING, AND OTHER FALSE ALARMS

This book is printed on acid-free paper.

Library of Congress Cataloging-in-Publication Data

Campbell, Ted.
The sky is falling, the church is dying, and other false alarms / Ted A. Campbell. — First [edition].
pages cm
Includes bibliographical references.
ISBN 978-1-4267-8594-8 (binding: soft back) 1. Christian sects—History. 2. Christianity—Forecasting. 3. End of the world—History of doctrines. I. Title.
BR157.C37 2015
277.3'083—dc23
2015019300

15 16 17 18 19 20 21 22 23 24—10 9 8 7 6 5 4 3 2 1
MANUFACTURED IN THE UNITED STATES OF AMERICA

CONTENTS

FOREWORD

Ted A. Campbell is crazy. Certifiable. Nuts. He doesn't think the sky is falling. He looks around at all the evidence, all the signs of the state of Protestant Christianity in the United States and dares to say, "The sky is not falling." Anyone who looks at the shape of traditional old-line Protestant churches will tell you that all the evidence points to the fact that, indeed, the sky is falling. Churches are dying. Denominations are declining rapidly. The sky is falling; but Ted doesn't believe it. Ted A. Campbell is just plain crazy. Or is he?

When I was elected bishop of the Northern Texas-Northern Louisiana Synod (Evangelical Lutheran Church in America) in 2000 I regularly heard claims that by the year 2025, 75 percent of Protestant churches in the United States would be closed. Coming from twenty years in parish ministry where I led two congregations in significant growth and building programs, I was going to be in the forefront of re-creating our denomination's churches so that we would show the world there is still life left in these old bones. Discipleship would be my theme. "Sowing and growing disciples of Jesus" would be our mission. DiscipleLife would be our brand. This would turn our denomination around; churches that were dying relics of the past would become vital, alive communities of faith. I was crazy, just like

Ted A. Campbell, except I was wrong and Ted is right. Perhaps it is all about expectations... realistic expectations... and an honest view of what the church is called to be. I wanted to re-create the past; Ted directs our eyes to the future.

Ted helps us understand that by measuring church life and faithful communities using the standards of the past—worship attendance, baptized members, Sunday school participants, or offerings for the work of national judicatory offices—we will find that the church has declined. The *institution* of the church is not what it used to be. Perhaps, Ted affirms, it never was what we thought it was, what we wished it was.

Culture has changed and the way we live our faith is changing. I got the focus right: discipleship, DiscipleLife; but I hoped for resurrection of the church I grew up loving. That just won't happen. The church is not the center of believers' lives as it used to be; the church is not the center of the community as it was in many places. The church is not the place to leverage social and business relationships as in the past. The church is much less the place to see and be seen. Thus, people attend worship much less frequently and Sunday school is practically dead. Yet, disciples profess faith and commitment to Jesus as Lord and they support their congregations when they are doing something relevant and life-changing for their communities. People are not joiners today; yet, when asked, they will say the church they attend monthly or a couple times a year is, indeed, their church.

Yes, some congregations have declined and closed within my judicatory over the past fifteen years, but just as many new starts have sprung up. Now, however, instead of worshipping in the traditional Lutheran languages of German, Norwegian, or Swedish, the languages of new mission starts among us Lutherans in the Dallas area are: Umoja (Tanzania), Oromo (Ethiopia), Indonesian (South Pacific), and Spanish. We learn from Philip Jenkins and others that Christianity still has the largest number of followers in the world and will remain in the lead through 2050 according to projections from the Pew Research Center. It is exploding in the southern hemisphere and Christians from those lands are looking to the United States as an opportunity for mission and outreach of the gospel. This points to a different kind of growth in the future.

Others point out that we have lost the youth and young adults; that those under thirty claim to be "spiritual, but not religious." While that may be true generally, I see outreach to youth and young adults as taking on new life. Twenty-first-century church leaders are seizing opportunities here through the practice of flash-mob Bible studies, exciting mission trips, and new ministries such as KYRIE PubChurch in Fort Worth. PubChurch is Sunday early evening worship in a restaurant/bar in a rejuvenating, eclectic neighborhood of Fort Worth. Music is shared by a different band each week (much of it old-time Gospel music), a scripture is read, a word is shared, and the Eucharist is offered for any and all in the place. Diners come for food or beverage or the football game on television and go home having worshipped and received the word. This growing community is going to be replicated in the Dallas-Fort Worth area as it is touching the lives of young adults. This may not become a large megachurch with lots of members on the rolls; but it is an expression of the changing church for changing times.

The 2005 book *Chasing Down a Rumor: The Death of the Mainline Denominations* by Lutherans Bob Bacher and Kenneth Inskeep was my first experience with the thought that the mainline is not really as dead in the water as people in popular and mainstream media like to point out. *The Sky Is Falling, the Church Is Dying, and Other False Alarms* by Ted A. Campbell takes their thoughts and pushes them deeper into the changing culture of the twenty-first century and helps us have conversation around the reality that the church, while not dying, is alive and changing. It is growing deeper in faith and care of others by those who still commit themselves to their local congregations, and it is much broader than church buildings.

Ted A. Campbell is crazy... crazy right and nuts about his faith. This is what continues to grow in our culture and as a result of our church's ministries. He's just crazy and thought provoking enough to guide Christians into deeper hope for the future of their church and our faith.

Rev. Dr. Kevin S. Kanouse, Bishop
Northern Texas-Northern Louisiana Mission Area (Synod)
Evangelical Lutheran Church

Chapter One

MYTHS

It's a bummer to wake up in the morning and hear that you're dead. But that's the way it has felt for folks in America's older Protestant churches for the last four decades. Yes, that means you, Lutherans and Presbyterians and UCC and Methodists and Episcopalians and even some Baptists. And Disciples of Christ. And Reformed Church in America folks. You're dying. Wait, that means me. We're dying. Actually, it's worse than that. Not only are we dying, we don't believe in Jesus. We're faithless. We're probably not even Christians any more. And we're mega-stupid because we don't even realize how dying and faithless we are.

Don't give me the drill about how you see signs of life and younger people in your congregations. Goody for you. But that doesn't matter. Popular opinion has already judged our churches and it doesn't matter what is actually happening in them. Judgment has been pronounced: dying, faithless, stupid. Even some folks in our churches seem to agree now.

To be clear: there's no doubt about the *decline* in overall memberships of historic Protestant churches and other religious groups in the United States. Since the turn of the twenty-first century, it increasingly appears that almost all traditional religious groups—including conservative evangelical churches and megachurches in the

United States, as well as the Catholic Church and other Protestant churches—are declining as a percentage of the US population. The persistent myth that we need to challenge head-on is the myth of the *demise* or *impending death* of "mainline" or old-line or ecumenically engaged Protestant churches in the United States. That's the myth I'm willing to take on in what follows. I'd like to contest the impression that we're unfaithful, stupid, and near death. I'd like to offer just a bit of sober encouragement to folks in these churches.

I am an elder of The United Methodist Church, a historian, and a long-time participant in inter-Christian dialogue. I usually write sedate prose about the "endorsements" of eighteenth-century letters or ecumenical consensus on the matter of Christ's presence in the Lord's Supper. The topic of this book engages my interests as a historian, but I confess that it raises my emotional temperature in a way that endorsements to eighteenth-century letters usually don't. I'm writing here as an engaged participant, not an embedded reporter.

A Challenging Idea

Just a little background. In 1972 a staff member at the National Council of the Churches of Christ in the USA, Dean M. Kelley, introduced a startling, original thesis in a book called *Why Conservative Churches Are Growing*. Kelley wasn't griping. He was telling the truth.

Folks in "mainline" churches (Kelley called them "ecumenical" Protestant churches) were stunned at Kelley's claim that "conservative" denominations and independent congregations in the United States were growing, and that older churches were losing ground to them at that time. Folks from the older churches reacted with scorn and dismissal. "Conservatives," they imagined, were stupid, uncultured turkeys who didn't keep up with the times. Only idiots would be attracted to their churches. Surely it was a blip, and the old-line, mainline churches with their beautiful sanctuaries and advanced cultures and progressive outlooks would come back and *kapow!* beat the stuffing out of these pretenders.

Well, the dust has cleared and Kelley was on target at least with respect to what was happening in his time. By the time he died in 1997, few scholars had been so thoroughly vindicated as he was with the possible exception of his near contemporary Peter Higgs. As in "Higgs boson." The groups Kelley called "conservative" churches were growing at that time. It's also true that they have begun to show signs of decline in relation to the US population since around the year 2000, and most of them that were growing in the previous thirty years had begun to look suspiciously "mainline" and a lot less fundamentalist than they did back in Kelley's time.

Kelley's book set the stage for discussions in historic US Protestant churches for the decades to come. Although seldom examined carefully, his research stimulated a pattern of repetitious writing that has grown like an out-of-control cancer into horrendous stereotyping and brutal, overt scorn for "mainline" churches in popular American culture, even on the part of members and leaders of our churches. A catastrophe of biblical proportions! The apocalypse come to our churches! Epic fail! Mythic fail! *Mythic* turns out to be an appropriate word.

The image of weak and declining churches has been carried forward in the last twenty years by news services in the United States, consistent with their general sense that religion itself is a dying relic of the past. Early in 2001, only one major US video news organization had a national-level religion reporter. That was ABC's *World News Tonight*, and they fired Peggy Wehmeyer without replacement a few months before the 9/11 attacks. Who needs a religion reporter? And after 9/11, the news feeds flooded us with images of hate-filled, bigoted Muslims and Christians. The public at large could easily gain the impression that this is what Islam and Christianity have always been about.

The image of weak and declining churches has been carried forward in the last twenty years by news services in the United States, consistent with their general sense that religion itself is a dying relic of the past.

News sources reported correctly in 2010 that there were no more Protestants on the US Supreme Court, a body that at one time consisted solely of Protestants. In October 2012 they reported that a majority of US citizens no longer identified themselves as Protestants. These developments were widely attributed to shrinkage of the old-line Protestant churches. Easy targets. It was scarcely noted that in this case, "Protestant" included conservative evangelical groups as well as the older, historic Protestant churches of the United States. Much bigger things were happening than the shrinkage of the older churches.

But the impression you'd gain from reading these news accounts is that if you attended an Episcopal or United Methodist or United

Church of Christ (UCC) or Presbyterian (PC[USA]) or Lutheran (ELCA) congregation today, you'd see mostly empty pews with a scattering of wrinkled-up old farts just about to die, barely able to keep the heat running in their decrepit sanctuaries while they argue with their faltering, halitosis-infected dying breaths about ordaining gay people. In a few months, they'll all croak and then there won't be any more Methodists or Presbyterians or Lutherans or UCC folk or Episcopalians to worry about. Uh oh. Put on the heart monitor. *beep* *beep* *beep* *bee-ee-ee-ee-eep* Flatline. Good riddance. Stupid, unfaithful, dying, dead and gone.

No, actually, it would be difficult to get even that impression from news sources, which largely ignore historic Protestant churches except, for example, when Chelsea Clinton marries a Jewish guy and Methodists get a throwaway line from talk-show host and comedian Jon Stewart: "Being a Methodist is easy. It's like the University of Phoenix of religion."

We do get attention from the news services when we argue about homosexuality. There must have been a memo sent to reporters that said, "You are strictly not to mention The UMC or the PC(USA) or the ELCA or the Episcopal Church in the USA or the United Church of Christ unless they are arguing about gay people." That's the only news story to them.

For the news feeds, "Christianity" now seems to mean fundamentalist Protestants and conservative Catholics, just as "Islam" denotes Islamic State terrorists hacking people's heads off. News stories feed on conflict, and middle-of-the-road religious groups don't supply near enough of it. So religious traditions have come to be viewed publicly in the light of their most conservative expressions—

sometimes their most hate-filled expressions—with the interesting exception of "Buddhism," which always seems to denote the warmest, fuzziest, non-ascetic flavors of the Buddhist tradition. Meanwhile, middle-of-the-road and more progressive Christians, Jews, and Muslims don't count, even if they have traditional beliefs. They're boring. They're not blowing up anything, just praying and worshipping and building hospitals and universities and opening clinics for poor people. *snore* What a bunch of losers!

US society at large has developed an image of our churches based on monstrously exaggerated rumors fed by news stories and only distantly grounded in Kelley's research. The truth is that they haven't got a clue what's going on in our churches, but they sure think they do, and they're very happy to share their immense wisdom about our failures. As we shall see.

Unoriginal Ideas

What really hasn't helped has been a series of books that have come out every few years since 1972 written mostly by people in historic Protestant denominations and whose content can be summarized as follows:

> WOW PEOPLE! HAVE I GOT SOME STUNNING NEWS FOR YOU! NOBODY HAS EVER THOUGHT OF THIS BEFORE! CONSERVATIVE CHURCHES ARE GROWING AND MAINLINE CHURCHES ARE DECLINING! YOU'RE DECLINING! YOU'RE GOING TO DIE! THE SKY IS FALLING! YOU'RE ALL IMBECILES! FAITHLESS IMBECILES! FAITHLESS, IMMORAL IMBECILES! NOBODY IS DOING ANYTHING ABOUT IT! IT'S HOR-

> RIBLE!! IT'S DEPRESSING!! IT'S DREADFUL!! AND I'M THE FIRST PERSON EVER TO SAY ANYTHING LIKE THIS!!

Something like that. And then a few years later, it's...

> WOW PEOPLE! HAVE I GOT SOME STUNNING NEWS FOR YOU! NOBODY HAS EVER THOUGHT OF THIS BEFORE! CONSERVATIVE CHURCHES ARE GROWING AND...

Wholly unoriginal, Batman! It was original in 1972 for Dean M. Kelley. Now it's just griping. And very unoriginal griping at that. Tell me something new.

US society at large has developed an image of our churches based on monstrously exaggerated rumors fed by news stories and only distantly grounded in research.

It's puzzling—just to take one example close to my own experience—for the three million people who worship at United Methodist congregations every week in the United States, people in large congregations, people in middle-sized suburban congregations, people in little white-frame rural churches, people in huge congregations that function as United Methodist megachurches, gay people, lesbian people, black people, white people, Latino people, and people who couldn't tell you if they're black or white or whatever to save their souls. It's puzzling for United Methodist people singing Charles

Wesley hymns and attending Walk to Emmaus retreats, Methodist camps, DISCIPLE Bible study groups, hymn sings, revivals, and the functional third Methodist sacrament of covered-dish suppers. It's especially puzzling for United Methodists in thriving congregations today who have to presume, based on the news feeds and the horror stories, that their congregation is the only exception to the rule and every other congregation in the denomination is decrepit and dying. But hey, that's what they're saying out there in pop culture and news feeds. Could news sources be wrong or mistaken or misleading even in the slightest degree? I mean, when they're reporting about religion?

"... Gone from the World of Christianity"

US Representative Rick Santorum has given us a provocative sound bite illustrating how some folks outside of our churches see us. Speaking at Ave Maria University in 2008 in what sounds in the audio recording like an off-the-cuff comment, the Catholic presidential hopeful declared, "And of course we look at the shape of mainline Protestantism in this country and it is in shambles, it is gone from the world of Christianity as I see it."

Thanks especially for that "of course." Of course! The conclusion is perfectly obvious to him. All of our churches are "gone from the world of Christianity." I think he meant that not only are we declining but also we've basically given up on Christian faith.

So Laura and George W. Bush regularly attend a United Methodist congregation, "gone from the world of Christianity." Barbara and George H. W. Bush and Colin and Alma Powell attend Episcopal churches, "gone from the world of Christianity." Condoleezza

Rice attends a Presbyterian church, "gone from the world of Christianity." And that's just considering a few folks within the fold of Rep. Santorum's own political party! Judgment has been pronounced!

And Rick Santorum is far from the only one who sees older Protestant churches in that way. Writing on "The Death of Protestant America" in *First Things* in the same year as Santorum's comment, Joseph Bottum made much more specific his sense that older churches have abandoned Christian faith:

> The names may vary, but the topics remain the same: the uniformity of social class at the church headquarters, the routine genuflections toward the latest political causes, the feminizing of the clergy, the unimportance of the ecclesial points that once defined the denomination, the substitution of leftist social action for Christian evangelizing, and the disappearance of biblical theology. All the Mainline churches have become essentially the same church: their histories, their theologies, and even much of their practice lost to a uniform vision of social progress. Only the names of the corporations that own their properties seem to differ.

"All the Mainline churches have become essentially the same church." Really? And what was the evidence for "the uniformity of social class at the church headquarters"? Wow. I missed that memo. I guess we are just wretched. And stupid. And faithless. Oh yeah, and dying. Stay tuned this evening for "The Death of Protestant America." *beep* *beep* *beep* *bee-ee-ee-ee-eep* Party time! Excellent!

These are astonishing judgments. We might hope that they were grounded in careful study of the doctrinal commitments and the liturgies and the ecumenical and social commitments of contemporary

Episcopal, Lutheran, Presbyterian, Disciples, UCC, AME, RCA, and United Methodist churches. I don't think so. They don't reveal that they know much about our churches at all despite the fact that they claim sufficient expertise to make these enormous public pronouncements. Looks like they just drank in whatever politicians and pop culture threw up about the hideous mainline churches and then spat it back out in a speech at Ave Maria University and in the pages of *First Things*.

You don't have to like it, but I think it's not just Rick Santorum and Joseph Bottum. I think that's what people are really thinking and saying out there. Our churches are "gone from the world of Christianity." You and me and the whole cast of characters who attend Methodist and UCC and Episcopal and Lutheran and Reformed Church in America and Disciples and Presbyterian churches.

In fact, it feels as though we're caught in a pincer movement from the outside. In this corner *bing* you have popular media who seem convinced that religion always means hate-filled bigotry, and we consistently disappoint them. No story. In the other corner *bing* you have flavors of contemporary American conservatism for whom our churches have taken far too progressive stances ("the feminizing of the clergy," *gasp*) for us to count as their kind of Christians. *bing* Let the fight begin. And we just stand there and let them clobber us from all sides. No, actually, what we do is clobber each other.

On the inside, the image of declining churches has given every special-interest group in our churches, and for that matter just about every individual with an opinion, grounds for saying that the decline is due to the fact that the churches haven't followed X, which of course denotes their own ideas or their program. One group in our churches—whether it's *bing* low-church conservative, *bing* socially progressive, *bing* charismatic, *bing* theologically liberal, or *bing* high-church conservative—acknowledges the facts about decline and blames it on other groups. Other groups . . . well, you can guess. Denominational meetings—trust me, I know what I'm talking about—easily devolve into gripe sessions about who's responsible for the decline of the churches, and the cardinal rule of a gripe session is: It's not me. It's not my group. It's someone else. It's "those people," whoever they are. *bing* Let the fight begin. Christ, have mercy upon us.

A Good Word for Historic Protestant Churches in the United States

Dead. Faithless. Stupid. Anybody got a good word out there? What follows is not an analysis of the decline of the older Protestant churches nor a program for their reformation. No, I'm not "seeing the world through rose-colored glasses" or crying "peace, peace" when there is no peace (Jer 6:14 NRSV). This is a post-apocalyptic message coming to you from the scorched earth and smoldering ruins of historic Protestant churches.

Even so, during and after the ecclesiastical apocalypse we ought to be "encouraging each other and building each other up" (1 Thess 5:11). That's what I'd like to do here for the twenty-five million or so Christians in older Protestant churches in the United States. I want to offer just a little sober encouragement in response to those who seem so eager to declare us dead.

The truth is that almost no one wants to claim the offensive term "mainline" these days. The only reason for using the expression here, or for talking about denominations, or for limiting this discussion to churches in the United States, for that matter, is that contemporary discussions of church decline and demise speak consistently of "mainline denominations" in the United States. As a historian, I'd prefer to use the terminology of historic Protestant churches or perhaps "old-line churches," that is, non-Catholic and non-Orthodox churches that originated from denominations and religious movements that date from the colonial period in US history or soon thereafter. Dean Kelley spoke of "ecumenical" Protestant churches, though some of the groups he described as "conservative churches" have become engaged with ecumenical dialogue since 1972. Historically black churches such as the AME, AME Zion, and CME churches have not been traditionally included among "mainline" churches, but they share most of the common characteristics of other historic Protestant churches in the United States.

The truth is that almost no one wants to claim the offensive term "mainline" these days.

Whether we include Baptist groups within the scope of old-line or historic Protestant churches comes down to a matter of particular criteria by which we define and understand historic Protestant ("mainline," "old-line") churches in contrast to evangelical Protestant communities. These are broadly overlapping categories, and Baptist congregations tend to be points of strong overlap. Using the criteria given below, I will consider the American Baptist Churches and the more recently formed Cooperative Baptist Fellowship within the scope of historic Protestant churches, and I'll consider the Southern Baptist Convention as more representative of the conservative evangelical pattern of US Protestantism. The truth is, however, that many particular congregations of the Southern Baptist Convention and the National Baptist conventions share much in common with old-line Protestant groups.

Despite their very different origins and their own distinctive traditions of Christian doctrines, practices, and spiritualities, the old-line and ecumenically engaged non-Catholic and non-Orthodox churches in the United States share several characteristics in common.

- These churches originated from denominations or religious movements that existed in North America from colonial times or shortly thereafter. This is the main criterion I've used to identify these churches. The Christian Church, Disciples of Christ, originated from an American religious movement in the early 1800s, though they had roots in Scots Presbyterian movements and have come to share characteristics with the other historic Protestant churches described here.
- Most of these churches have formal doctrinal standards and authorized liturgies (forms of worship) that reflect a common inheritance of Western Christian culture.
- These church bodies were either divided over issues of race and slavery in the 1800s or, in the case of AME, AME Zion, and CME churches, they originated out of contexts of racial segregation and mistreatment based on race.
- These groups have had basically two forms of conservatism: an evangelical ("low-church," conversionist) subculture, as

well as a "high-church" subculture oriented toward sacramental celebration in continuity with ancient and medieval practices. I see your dubious looks out there. Stick with me. I'm serious.

- These churches have been influenced by streams of Protestant liberalism in the twentieth century, and they have tolerated various flavors of liberal theology in theological schools and among clergy, though it has not influenced the formal doctrinal or liturgical commitments of the churches to the degree that's often alleged. Moreover, theologians and theological schools associated with these churches have also been influenced by the Neo-Orthodox theological movement and conservative theological movements of the twentieth century.
- These churches took progressive stands on social issues in the twentieth century, including their engagement with the civil rights movement and the feminist movement.
- These church groups, with the possible exception of the AME Zion Church, have shown significant decline in overall membership since the 1960s, and a smaller degree of decline in church attendance, though as we will see, attendance declines have not been as steep as the decline of overall membership numbers. We will also see that statistics show some unexpected, residual strengths in these churches. STARTLING NEWS: a few of the historic Protestant churches will probably still exist even by the time you finish reading this book.
- These church bodies have been actively engaged in the ecumenical movement of the twentieth century, and through the ecumenical movement, most of these churches have formally recognized each other as churches that share the gospel, and have enacted a complex web of inter-church agreements for sharing ministries and sacraments with each other.

These characteristics describe at least twelve denominations that I include among historic Protestant churches in the United States:

- The African Methodist Episcopal (AME) Church
- The African Methodist Episcopal Zion (AME Zion) Church
- American Baptist Churches (ABC)
- The Christian Church, Disciples of Christ
- The Christian Methodist Episcopal (CME) Church
- The Cooperative Baptist Fellowship (CBF)
- The Episcopal Church in the USA (ECUSA)
- The Evangelical Lutheran Church in America (ELCA)
- The Presbyterian Church (U.S.A.) (PC[USA])
- The Reformed Church in America (RCA)
- The United Church of Christ (UCC)
- The United Methodist Church (UMC)

I'm also inclined to include within the range of historic Protestant churches many of the groups that have divided in recent decades from these denominations. Really? Yes, really. For example, a group of Lutheran congregations separated from the ELCA in the last five years over their opposition to the denomination's provision for the ordination of homosexual persons. But this group of churches continues to ordain women and shows most of the characteristics of the historic denominations named here. The same would probably apply to Anglican congregations that have severed ties with the ECUSA and aligned themselves with other Anglican provinces. In a large-scale view, these divisions have not changed the overall numbers of historic Protestant church participants; they're just divided into a few more groups today.

Chapter Two

FACTS

The myth is that we're faithless imbeciles in dying churches. And it's not just people outside of our churches who believe that. A lot of folks in our churches seem to have internalized that image of ourselves. But what's really happening? There's no doubt about the reality of decline in overall membership and weekly attendance, as we will see. But demise or impending death is another issue. That's what I want to contest in what follows.

This has required me to make a foray into the world of contemporary church statistics, an alien world for most historians. But the statistics I will share serve as markers of historical trends, and I mean to interpret them as a historian. It's important to understand not only the statistics about membership and attendance but also to understand critical presuppositions that interpreters bring to them. For example, the presupposition that the historic Protestant churches dominated American religious life early in the twentieth century. Starting with this one, here are four facts worth noting about old-line churches in the United States, followed by One Big Fact.

Fact One

Fact one: historic Protestant churches were never the dominant center of American religion they're supposed to have been in the twentieth century.

The story of "mainline decline" is well known, so hackneyed by now that Martin Marty has suggested that we reduce it to the single word MainlineDecline. The standard narrative goes something like this: America's mighty mainline Protestant churches once stretched from sea to shining sea, embracing the vast majority of American people who worshipped week after week, piously filling glorious churches with their hymns of praise, but now they are reduced to a grim handful of decrepit pensioners rapidly dying off. The impression you're supposed to get is that in a few months they'll all be gone. *beep* *beep* *beep* *bee-ee-ee-ee-eep*

That's the story. But this way of telling the story has a seriously flawed presupposition. Just how mighty were the historic Protestant churches in the United States at the beginning of the twentieth century?

The Association of Religion Data Archives (ARDA), a funded project based at Penn State University, offers statistics on most US religious communities going back to 1925. These membership statistics paint a very different picture of American denominational life in the twentieth century than the picture so often presumed in the standard telling of mainline declension since the 1960s. In what follows, I'll examine their US church membership figures according to the ARDA at twenty-five-year intervals, in 1925, 1950, 1975, and 2000. However, the ARDA figures have to be used with caution.

- The ARDA does not have sustained statistics for the Christian Methodist Episcopal (CME) Church and the African Methodist Episcopal (AME) Church, though it does have comparable statistics for other denominations considered here as older Protestant churches.
- The Cooperative Baptist Fellowship (CBF) became separate from the Southern Baptist Convention in the early 1990s, and we cannot track predecessor groups for them as we can in other cases. It would give a false impression to include their membership data (only for the year 2000) in a table like this. Subtracting the AME and CME churches and the CBF, then, we have nine denominations for which there are consistent ARDA statistics from 1925 through 2000.
- Almost every one of these contemporary historic Protestant denominations had a complex history of unions—and a few divisions—through the twentieth century. So The United Methodist Church can be found under that name in 1975 and 2000. But in 1950, one has to add together the membership of two predecessor denominations: The Methodist Church and The Evangelical United Brethren Church. And back in 1925 these two denominations were represented by five distinct groups: The Evangelical Association, the Church of the United Brethren in Christ, The Methodist Episcopal Church, The Methodist Episcopal Church, South, and The Methodist Protestant Church. It's even more fun for Lutherans, who seem to have had a separate Evangelical Lutheran synod on every other street corner in Minneapolis in 1925. Actually I count nine groups as the 1925 predecessors of today's Evangelical Lutheran Church in America.

- The ARDA data in some cases do not correspond to figures used internally by denominational groups today. PC(USA) statistics, for example, show their membership in recent decades in the range of two million members; the ARDA data show their membership in the range of three million members. It may be that one is using the number of baptized members and the other is using the number of confirmed members, which is bound to be smaller.

With these cautions in mind, we can put it all together and end up with a table showing the following membership figures for oldline churches from ARDA data at the intervals 1925, 1950, 1975, 2000:

Total Membership	1925	1950	1975	2000
American Baptist Churches	1,464,167	1,561,073	1,603,033	1,436,909
AME Zion Church	490,000	530,116	1,054,182	1,296,662
Christian Church, Disciples	1,441,462	1,767,964	1,302,164	820,286
Episcopal Church USA	1,164,911	2,417,464	2,857,513	2,333,327
ELCA	1,702,015	4,063,480	5,496,888	5,125,919
Presbyterian Church (U.S.A.)	2,454,647	3,256,128	3,535,825	3,485,332
Reformed Church in America	145,373	183,178	355,052	289,392

United Church of Christ	1,662,674	1,977,418	1,818,762	1,377,320
United Methodist Church	7,835,648	9,653,178	9,957,710	8,340,954
TOTAL	18,360,897	25,409,999	27,981,129	24,506,101
US population	114,612,114	151,325,798	214,878,865	281,421,906
Percent of US population	16.0	16.8	13.0	8.7

Perhaps this isn't all of the historic, ecumenically oriented Protestant churches. It doesn't include the AME and CME denominations or the Cooperative Baptist Fellowship because comparable statistical data from 1925 to 1950 are lacking for them. Perhaps there are a few others, but who would they be? Perhaps the National Baptist churches and the Lutheran Church, Missouri Synod. But I think it's accurate to say that these nine groups represent a strong core of historic Protestant churches in the United States.

So here's the deal. The figures given here show that *these nine denominations and their predecessors never accounted for more than 16.8 percent of the US population* in the period (1925–2000) for which we have sustained, comparable statistics. This is hardly the powerhouse center of American religion depicted in standard narratives of decline. Even if you were to add some more groups and presuppose that the percentage was higher before 1925, I doubt that the membership of these churches ever accounted for more than a quarter of the US population in the twentieth century.

The table shows that the percentage of members of these churches compared to the rapidly growing US population fell significantly since 1950. This change can be tied most consistently to trends in immigration to the United States in which non-Protestant groups constituted the great majority of newer immigrants since the late 1800s. Diana Eck has shown that these trends accelerated as a result of the Immigration and Nationality Act of 1965.

The question is how these churches came to be considered the mighty American "mainline" if they did not statistically represent anything close to a majority of Americans?

So *how did these churches come to be considered the mighty American "mainline"* if they did not statistically represent anything close to a majority of Americans? It's a complicated story that involves at least the following elements.

- The distant memory of a time—prior to the Civil War—when Methodists, Baptists, Lutherans, Episcopalians, Congregationalists, and Presbyterians probably did constitute a majority of non-Catholic Americans, if not of Americans as a whole
- The corresponding cultural impression that these churches were the "truly American" churches in contrast with other Christian groups (Catholic and Orthodox churches) and Jewish groups still associated with immigrant communities in the early twentieth century

- The engagement of these churches in the quasi-governmental Federal Council of Churches in the United States, the predecessor of the National Council of the Churches of Christ that was empowered by the US government to allocate religious broadcasting slots for radio and television

It's not surprising that in the early twentieth century, the term "mainline" would become a favored way to describe these churches, evoking the wealth and privilege of the affluent suburbs of Philadelphia clustered along the "main line" of railways that led out west from the heart of the city.

It's also not surprising that older Protestant churches would have attracted a substantial number of nominal members, attracted by the sheen of mainline respectability but hardly catechized and barely if at all committed to historic Christian faith and practices. The membership figures given above *do not show a consistent decline in membership* between 1925 and 2000. Rather, they show *a bulge in membership* that peaked in the mid to late 1960s. It now appears that this was not a pregnant bulge. It was more like a cancerous growth constituted by a host of nominal church members now rapidly disappearing from membership statistics as they die off. To his great credit as an observer, Dean Kelley keenly recognized the problems inherent in nominal church membership. His passionate concern through his book was not simply with the statistical decline of the ecumenical churches but to name the qualitative issues that an easygoing approach to church membership posed for them.

So what's left after the fashionable, nominal old-line church members of the mid-twentieth century fade away? Probably neither the mythical mighty American mainline that never was, nor the wretched handful of wrinkled-up old farts waiting to die that popular reports have depicted. These figures suggest that historic Protestant churches had an exaggerated sense of their own importance in the early twentieth century, and that false memory of glory days in a mythical past continues to haunt us as we wonder why we're not "mainline" any more. News Flash: We never were.

Moreover, it's important to notice that evangelical churches, including the well-known evangelical megachurches, have begun to show signs of decline in recent years in contrast to their growth in the 1980s and 1990s. A 2012 Pew Center study of religion and public life showed that the percentage of Americans who identified themselves as evangelicals or "born again" Christians declined from 21 percent in 2007 to 19 percent five years later in 2012. A subsequent study in 2015 confirmed this trend. The notion that "mainline churches are declining and evangelical churches are growing" does not seem to be holding into the twenty-first century. This suggests that there is a new or newly resurgent factor of secularization affecting all US religious communities.

It's worth saying in the wake of rumors of our demise that the information above shows that these denominations ended the twentieth century with six million more members than they had in 1925, and probably a whole lot more than they had in 1900.

It's worth saying in the wake of rumors of our demise that the information above shows that these denominations ended the twentieth century with six million more members than they had in 1925, and probably a whole lot more than they had in 1900. If this is supposed to represent a cataclysmic, apocalyptic, biblical-scale catastrophe for historic Protestant churches, then I have to tell you I'm not very impressed. *yawn* Really, I was expecting something a lot more dramatic than that. The numbers are consistent with decline. They're nowhere close to death or demise. *beep* *beep* *beep* *beep*

Fact Two

Fact two: historic Protestant churches, parallel to other religious groups in the United States, have shown declines in weekly attendance in the later twentieth century and beyond.

Weekly attendance figures in historic Protestant churches have also shown declines in recent decades and in fact a sharper decline since the year 2000. There is not a source of consistent weekly attendance data as there is for membership data from the ARDA, but I have gathered data from four of the largest of the old-line denominations (United Methodist Church, Evangelical Lutheran Church in America, Presbyterian Church (U.S.A.), and the Episcopal Church in the USA) from 1990 to the present. These show average weekly attendance numbers as follows:

	1990	1995	2000	2005	2010
ECUSA	823,384	828,049	908,971	787,271	657,831
ECLA	1,636,860	1,571,680	1,566,993	1,439,710	1,186,099
PC(USA)	1,244,173	1,212,024	1,190,801	1,089,006	926,303
UMC	3,466,439	3,428,708	3,487,629	3,344,488	3,053,120
TOTAL	7,170,856	7,040,461	7,154,394	6,660,475	5,823,353

These figures show that average weekly worship attendance for these four denominations closely paralleled each other in this period. Despite declines in membership, weekly attendance remained virtually flat through the 1990s—it actually rose between 1995 and 2000—and dropped off after the year 2000. What do we make of this? One thing is that weekly attendance figures have ceased to be the significant measure of active church membership that they once were. We'll take that up as a separate topic in the next section. Here we can consider some factors in the historical background of these weekly attendance figures.

In the first place, religious attendance in the United States has declined across the range of religious groups in the last forty years. Until quite recently, scholars reported that average weekly attendance at religious services in the United States had remained at about 40 percent of the population from the middle of the twentieth century through the present time. If that were the case, then attendance figures in historic Protestant churches would show us as mega losers. But pastors and other church leaders across a range of denominations knew that the 40 percent figure could not be accurate. I heard a Scottish theologian in Oxford state in the late 1970s that 50 percent of the population of Houston, Texas, attended church every Sunday. Having lived in Houston just before moving to Oxford, I knew that could not be the case. It wasn't.

It turns out that these statistics were based on polls that *asked participants* how often they attend church, and guess what? It turns out that folks were a little more pious but not as honest as one might have hoped. Studies based on *actual attendance numbers kept by churches*, as opposed to what people *say* they do, show that by 2010, overall worship attendance in all religious groups was down to about 21 percent in the United States. Scholars attribute the difference to what they call the "halo effect," that is, people *represent* themselves as active worshippers even when they may not have been for decades. That may sound somewhat less than encouraging for church folks, but it has an important implication: declines in old-line Protestant participation fall below the decline in overall religious participation in the United States from around 40 percent of the population in the 1950s to the present when only about 21 percent of the population participates weekly in worship.

A historian can also see in these figures the passing of "The Greatest Generation" of Americans, a generation well represented in historic Protestant churches, characterized by strong "joinerism," including unusually regular attendance at civic as well as religious gatherings. My own parents, of that generation, both born in 1926, attended church and other civic gatherings with intense regularity and taught their children to do likewise. They both died in 2011, but they had been unable to attend church regularly for some years prior to then. Multiply them times that whole wonderful generation shaped by the Depression and World War II, and you can envision the passing of a cloud of witnesses whose staunch devotion to church and civic institutions—yes, institutions—shamed those who went before them as well as those of us who follow them.

Moreover, I don't doubt at all that highly publicized controversies over gay unions and gay ordinations and intensive reporting about these controversies have had a negative effect on church activity since the 1980s. This does not mean, as it's sometimes reported, that old-line Christians are now flocking to evangelical churches.

There are individual cases, sometimes cases of which people are keenly aware, but statistical studies such as those examined by Mark Chaves in *American Religion: Contemporary Trends* (2011) show that the constituencies of newer evangelical churches seldom come from the ranks of active members of historic Protestant churches. And there are "defections" both ways.

Fact Three

Fact three: Weekly church attendance figures in historic Protestant churches have declined at a slower rate than overall membership figures, suggesting that the preponderance of lost membership has been of inactive members. Attendance patterns in recent decades also suggest that numbers of active members of congregations are higher than weekly attendance figures reveal.

A notable fact here is that weekly attendance figures do not parallel the overall membership figures. Attendance numbers have declined at a slower rate than church membership. One of the most fallacious presuppositions in recent discussions has been the notion that if a denomination loses two million members, then two million people who went to church before are no longer doing so. *snicker* Pastors and anyone else familiar with church life will now please pick themselves up off the floor after laughing their heads off at that piece of delicious fantasy. No, dear sweet peeps, the loss of two million members does *not* mean the loss of two million people who used to go to church regularly. But God bless your sweet, naïve, innocent souls for thinking that all members of churches regularly attend church.

The four denominations shown in the table on page 25—Episcopal, Lutheran (ELCA), Presbyterian (PC[USA]), and United

Methodist—declined 22 percent in combined membership in the twenty years between 1990 and 2010. Their average weekly combined worship attendance declined about 19 percent in the same twenty-year period. If we were to extend these figures over a longer period, we'd find that the decline in worship attendance is a consistently shallower decline than the decline in church memberships. In The United Methodist Church, for example, in the longer interval between 1976 and 2010, membership declined 23 percent and weekly attendance declined 16 percent. Anyone want to venture a wild guess that the difference between the membership loss and the smaller loss in weekly attendance meant a loss of inactive members?

It doesn't take a divine revelation to figure out what's going on here, though I'm always praying for one. Back in the 1940s, '50s, and even early '60s, being a member of a church or some other religious congregation was a norm in American society, whether people attended or not. Wake up and smell the coffee. It's no longer a social norm to belong to a religious group. *alarm* Really, I hate to tell you this, but belonging to a church is probably not going to help your social standing at all these days. But get this: after the loss of the fluff membership, *those who actually participate in their churches are now a stronger percentage of overall church membership* than they were forty years ago. Really.

After the loss of the fluff membership, those who actually participate in their churches are now a stronger percentage of overall church membership than they were forty years ago.

Speaking of fluff membership, it's pretty easy to see that nominal Methodists or Episcopalians or other old-line Protestants in the 1940s through the 1960s were pretty similar to the often-discussed group described as "nones" today, that is, people who now list their religious preference as "none" or religiously "unaffiliated." What's the difference between yesterday's inactive church members and today's "nones"? Let's see:

- Inactive church members in the 1940s, '50s, and '60s did not attend church; the "nones" today do not attend church.
- Inactive church members did not show outward signs of Christian discipleship; the "nones" today do not show outward signs of Christian discipleship.
- Inactive church members did not contribute to churches; the "nones" today do not contribute to churches.

Really, the only difference is that in the 1940s and '50s and '60s the names of inactive members were on the rolls of churches, and the "nones" today are not on the rolls of churches. The practical difference it's making in church life is about zero. It's just that the "nones" are more honest than yesterday's inactive church members.

Weekly attendance figures no longer reveal the level of church activity they once did. Why? Once upon a time in a galaxy far, far away, active church members came to church every Sunday. It wasn't really that far, far away: it was Beaumont, Texas, every Sunday when I was growing up there. But it seems like a long, long ago and far, far away kind of thing now.

The statistics for "average weekly worship attendance" are deeply problematic if they are taken as indicating how many active members churches have today. Average weekly attendance would indicate the number of active members only if active members attended weekly. There was a time when that was generally true, at the middle of the twentieth century. There was a time, for example, when public schools would not schedule soccer practices or other activities on Sunday mornings in deference to Christian worship customs. Those days are long past.

Pastors and other church leaders can tell you that lots of active churchgoers today attend less often, perhaps twice a month as opposed to weekly. I have to admit that I don't have a good source of data on how often church members attend today. I am forced at this point to rely on more impressionistic information, but what I hear consistently from pastors and other leaders, and what I see in congregations I attend and visit, is that a large number of active church members today do not attend weekly.

The overall number of active members—defined, say, as those who attend church at least twice monthly—will be considerably larger than the average weekly attendance figures.

This means that *the overall number of active members*—defined, say, as those who attend church at least twice monthly—*will be considerably larger than the average weekly attendance figures*. Stop and think about that for a minute. The frequency of attendance has declined. That's not a positive thing in itself, but it means that the overall numbers of active members of our churches are higher than the numbers for average weekly worship. Some have even argued that, due to this phenomenon, the overall numbers of active members today might even be higher than they were forty years ago. This points once again to a strong core of committed membership, stronger than represented in weekly attendance figures and stronger than has been depicted in popular accounts about our decline and demise. *beep* *beep* *beep* *beep*

Fact Four

Fact four: divisions in historic Protestant churches won't really change any of these large-scale facts.

HORROR! CATASTROPHE! PROTESTANT CHURCHES ARE DIVIDING! I'm a historian. *snore* You're going to have to work a lot harder than that to impress me. Yes, I know it feels dreadful, especially if you're having to figure out how to divide up church property and pension funds, but believe me: it isn't a novel situation.

Up to the beginning of the twentieth century, Protestant groups were dividing like amoebae. Just for the record, here's the list of twenty-eight denominations or mini-denominations in the year 1925 that I count as direct predecessors of the twelve historic Protestant denominations I have described in this book:

The African Methodist Episcopal Church
The African Methodist Episcopal Zion Church
The Christian Methodist Episcopal Church
The United Presbyterian Church of North America
The Presbyterian Church in the USA

The Presbyterian Church in the US
The Evangelical Synod of North America
The German Reformed Church [the one in the United States]
The Congregational Church
The [New England] Christian Churches [not to be confused with . . .]
The Christian Church, Disciples of Christ
The Methodist Protestant Church
The Methodist Episcopal Church
The Methodist Episcopal Church, South
The Evangelical Association
The Church of the United Brethren in Christ
The Episcopal Church (in the USA)
The United Lutheran Church of America
The Danish Evangelical Lutheran Church [the one in the United States]
The Augustana Synod [Lutheran]
The Finnish Evangelical Lutheran Church [the one in the United States]
The Norwegian Lutheran Church [the one in the United States]
The United Danish Evangelical Lutheran Church [the one in the United States]
The Iowa Synod [Lutheran]
The Ohio Synod [Lutheran]
The Buffalo Synod [Lutheran]
The Reformed Church in America
The Northern Baptist Churches

So consider the Church of What's Happening Now that once had 200 members. They divide into two rival groups: the Church of What's Happening Now, Old Constitution (124 members) and the

Church of What's Happening Now, New Light (76 members). Does that change the number of What's Happening Now Christians? Not really. Now they worship in two locations, and obviously 124 of them don't have the New Light, which really is a Big Deal for the 76 New Light folks. But the overall church membership stays about the same. Attendance stays about the same. Multiply that times a few million and you get a scenario like today's historic Lutheran and Anglican and Reformed and Baptist and Methodist churches in the United States.

One Big Fact

One Big Fact: historic Protestant churches today have a strong core of committed believers.

So here's the big deal. Those of us familiar with the life of congregations in historic Protestant churches know that *there is a strong core of committed believers in our churches, despite all the claims that have been made to the contrary*. The claims were grounded partly in a false sense of our own strength earlier in the twentieth century. Leaders of old-line churches exaggerated claims of their "mainline" status, and in the end those exaggerations returned to haunt us. In some cases the exaggerations result from misunderstandings described in this chapter about church membership and weekly attendance and their relevance to discerning active membership. In the next chapter I will show some qualitative ways in which our constituencies have been strengthened in recent years, for example, in stronger requirements for Christian formation and Christian profession.

There is a strong core of committed believers in our churches, despite all the claims that have been made to the contrary.

I'm not trying be Pollyanna here. Historic Protestant churches and other religious communities in the United States face serious problems today including declines in membership, weekly attendance, and the numbers of younger people attracted to our churches. But there is a significant core of active membership in our churches, and it is much, much stronger than we're represented as having by our contemporaries. Most people in our churches know this intuitively. They see younger generations of church members taking up the ways of being Christian that previous generations in their denominational families have held. They see continuing, strong membership and strong support in old-line churches. So I take back what I said at the beginning. It really *does* matter that you see younger people and signs of life in your congregations. *beep* *beep* *beep* *beep*

Chapter Three

LEGACIES

Myths abound about our churches. Facts and historical understanding behind the facts show that the older Protestant communities of the United States have a stronger core of faithful members than are often recognized. By way of offering encouragement, I want to describe some of the strengths of our churches, beginning with the historic legacies that we bring into the present.

Americans struggle with historic legacies, sometimes seeing the past as fetters that bind us. The Great Seal of the United States has the inscription NOVUS ORDO SECLORUM, somewhat dubiously spelled Latin for "a new order of ages." That is: We're doing something new and different here in America! Away with the past!! On to the future!!! A "new order of ages" starts here!!!! We can spell Latin any way we want to!!!!!

Protestant life in the United States has repeatedly involved religious leaders claiming that they have rediscovered the true Christian faith. Over and over again. It's like every Christian leader after the death of the last apostle screwed up and didn't comprehend the True Gospel because of their wickedness, but the Holy Spirit and I have at last found the True Gospel of Jesus. Right here in southwestern Kansas. And we have now established the One True Gospel of Jesus

Church and this is *not* another denomination or an institution; it is just the One True Gospel of Jesus Church, end of story.

But it's not really the end of the story because the One True Gospel of Jesus Church divides after a generation of leadership into the One True Gospel of Jesus Church, Reformation of 1912, and *The* One True Gospel of Jesus Church, Reformation of 1926, and they become competing denominations on the American scene.

And then someone else comes along and says, well, they completely missed the True Gospel of Jesus and the Holy Spirit and I have now discovered the True Gospel right here in southeastern Colorado. For heaven's sake, how could those Kansas people understand anything? And . . . you get the picture.

Part of the culture or ethos of historic Protestant churches is a somewhat more open attitude toward the possibility that the Holy Spirit was acting before the founding of our own churches, maybe even *cymbal crash* before we got to America. We have distinctive legacies as churches, but our legacies, the Christian cultures that we bring to the future, are a great part of our strength. We grow from our roots, and we have deep roots. I want to offer a little sober encouragement to Christians in historic Protestant churches by describing some of the strengths of our legacies. And contrary to almost everything else I do as a historian, I'm going to describe these strengths that arise out of our past in reverse chronological order.

Legacy One: Ecumenical Engagement and Commitments

The older Protestant churches of the United States built strong alliances with each other as a result of the ecumenical movement that flourished in the twentieth century. The Holy Spirit had some surprises for us and we did not end up with the monolithic super-church that some envisioned at the middle of the twentieth century, but we have built a set of strong and formally defined relationships with each other.

The ecumenical movement had brought these churches into much more direct contact with each other than they had experienced in the past. The ecumenical movement seeks the *visible unity* of churches in contrast to the *visible disunity* that has been so apparent in our histories. But historic Protestant churches had engaged in some collaborative work in the nineteenth century, for example, collaboration in missionary work, in producing common Sunday school literature, and in printing Bibles and tracts. By the end of the nineteenth century, such organizations as the YMCA and the YWCA, designed to help young people moving to take jobs in America's growing cities, offered further ventures for collaboration. Student Christian groups on college and university campuses offered yet another ground for common work. The Student Christian Movement, in particular, had taken up the lofty goal of "the evangelization of the world in this generation," and a new generation of well-educated American Protestants began to question whether traditional denominational divisions were helpful or necessary.

The ecumenical movement seeks the* visible unity *of churches in contrast to the* visible disunity *that has been so apparent in our histories.

The historic Protestant churches of the United States participated enthusiastically in ecumenical ventures in the early decades of the twentieth century. As early as 1908 their predecessor churches had formed the Federal Council of Churches in the USA. This group became the National Council of the Churches of Christ (NCCC) in the USA in 1956. All of the historic Protestant denominations discussed here are participants in the work of the NCCC. They have also been engaged in international ecumenical ventures, including the following areas of participation:

- Collaborative work in missions as a result of Edinburgh World Missionary Conference of 1910 that led to the formation of the International Missions Council (IMC)
- Collaborative work in Christian social outreach as a result of the first international conference on Life and Work held in Stockholm in 1925
- Collaborative discussions of church-dividing issues of doctrine and church polities as a result of the first international conference on Faith and Order held in Lausanne in 1927
- Collaborative work and discussions as a result of membership in the World Council of Churches (WCC) formed in 1948 and based on the early Life and Work movement and the earlier Faith and Order movement. The International Missions Council was eventually incorporated into the work of the WCC.

Although dreams of a large-scale multilateral union of churches were not realized in the twentieth century, a series of bilateral and multilateral discussions have led to formal relationships between these churches, allowing for full recognition of ministries and sacraments between most of them, and for the interchangeability of clergy within restrictions set out in particular agreements between churches. In the later decades of the twentieth century, the Evangelical Lutheran Church in America became the pioneer of these bilateral relationships and a central hub to which other historic Protestant denominations have been connected like spokes of a wheel. Historic Protestant churches in the United States ended the twentieth century with strong ties to each other and a growing sense of ecumenical consensus about the core of Christian faith that has been handed down to us.

Legacy Two: Postmillennial Optimism and Social Engagement

Back up a few decades. The early ecumenical movement was an outgrowth of a particular form of Protestant progressivism in the late 1800s and the early 1900s. A preponderance of American Protestants in this period believed that the second coming of Jesus would not occur until a long period of progress on earth had passed. Christ's kingdom would come on earth when the world itself had been thoroughly sanctified and prepared: "thy kingdom come, thy will be done on earth, as it is in heaven." Protestants in this age read biblical passages about the millennium, the thousand-year period spoken of in Revelation 20:1-6, as referring to this long period of progress. Christ would come after (*post-*) the millennium, so this progressive outlook is described as "postmillennial."

Progressive Christians in the mid-1800s weren't particularly worried about exactly when Jesus would return, because they recognized that the world was not close to being ready. Instead, they emphasized missionary work, evangelism, building schools and universities and hospitals, and developing clinics and shelters for the poor as ways of preparing the world for the coming reign of Christ. Such causes as the abolition of slavery and temperance in the use of alcoholic beverages were all seen as part of the postmillennial progressive outlook that characterized historic Protestant churches in the United States.

The decade of the 1890s witnessed a strong reaction against the optimistic, socially progressive postmillennial outlook. The Chicago evangelist D. L. Moody followed other conservative evangelical biblical scholars who argued that Christ would return before (*pre-*) the biblical millennium. Moody's "premillennial" outlook held that the world would be plunged into chaos after the return of Christ. It encouraged intense scrutiny of biblical passages like those in Daniel and the Revelation and St. Mark 13 and St. Matthew 25 about the return of Christ, and dissed progressive social work, seeing it as useless in the face of the coming dissolution of worldly institutions. Only evangelism and faith in Christ offered believers the possibility of escaping the calamities that were (they believed) soon to come.

Combined with opposition to modern scientific discoveries like Darwin's theory of evolution, and with a growing emphasis on the literal and unfailing meaning of the Bible for history and science, this outlook spawned modern fundamentalism. Some Presbyterians and Baptists were attracted to fundamentalism in the late 1800s and the early 1900s, and fundamentalism also spawned a multitude of newer Christian communities. Episcopalians, Lutherans, Methodists, and other Presbyterians and Baptists remained committed to a postmillennial vision of Christian progress.

The truth is that most of those who favored postmillennial progressivism maintained rather traditional theologies. By the late nineteenth century, some American theologians, especially those trained in Europe, had come to espouse truly modern or liberal theological views in addition to the socially progressive views that had long been espoused in the postmillennial outlook. Though historic Protestant churches may have tolerated liberal opinions on the part of its members and leaders, they did not typically institutionalize these liberal views by altering their traditional doctrines or liturgies.

Though historic Protestant churches may have tolerated liberal opinions on the part of its members and leaders, they did not typically institutionalize these liberal views by altering their traditional doctrines or liturgies.

Some scholars of American religious history have described what they call a "two-party system" in American Protestant culture in the early twentieth century, where the two parties were supposedly the fundamentalist evangelicals with their world-denying, premillennial outlook, and the progressive Protestants who espoused liberal theological views and progressive outlooks on social issues. I find that analysis very problematic. It disses conservatives within the historic Protestant churches. More specifically, it disses conservatives of the high-church flavor. Most problematically, it fails to distinguish between theological progressivism and social progressivism.

These did not always run together in the old-line churches, and in fact they do not today. The notion of a "two-party system" plays into those who espouse conspiracy theories in our churches by lumping all "conservatives" together and by lumping all "progressive" or "liberal" church folks together. That just doesn't work. Very typically, church leaders held theologically conservative views and espoused progressive attitudes toward social issues.

Here's an example. In the late 1800s, many American Protestants began to be concerned about the plight of immigrant communities moving into the larger cities of the United States, such as New York and Chicago. The Methodist Episcopal laywoman Lucy Rider Meyer (1849–1922) began working in the inner city of Chicago in the 1880s among immigrant women. She founded the Chicago Training School for City, Home, and Foreign Missions, and eventually developed an order of deaconesses in the Methodist Episcopal Church based on ancient and modern orders of deaconesses she described in a richly documented book on the subject. Lucy Rider Meyer had worked with the Chicago evangelist D. L. Moody early on, but Moody's premillennial outlook and his reticence to engage in concrete inner-city social work clashed with Meyer's postmillennial commitment to social action. Her theological outlook was very traditional though not fundamentalist, and her social engagement was quite progressive.

Perhaps the best-known expression of postmillennial social progressivism in the early twentieth century was the social gospel movement. Espoused by pastors and social activists in the growing cities of the United States in the early 1900s, the social gospel movement advocated concrete Christian involvement with the plight of the urban poor, including Christian intervention in labor disputes, advocacy on behalf of working conditions, opposition to child labor, and advocacy of at least a one-day reprieve from work in each week. Although it's sometimes dismissed as being hopelessly mired in liberal theologies, I am convinced that the earliest advocates of the social gospel, such as the Baptist pastor Walter Rauschenbusch in New York City, were following the older line of evangelical postmillennialism, now applied to the rather new and challenging situations of early twentieth-century cities. By the later decades of the twentieth century there were alliances between liberal theologians and social gospel advocates, but liberal theology has not been the only ground for progressive social involvement. Not by a long shot.

In the 1950s and the 1960s, historic Protestant churches in the United States generally supported the civil rights movement and sometimes took controversial stands in favor of civil rights legislation. The "Letter from a Birmingham Jail" of Rev. Dr. Martin Luther King Jr. was addressed to a specific group of southern church leaders who supported a gradual resolution of civil rights issues. Dr. King's message to them was to explain why their insistence on gradual change amounted to a cowardly denial of the need for immediate action to ensure civil rights.

But despite the social and political conservatism of some of their church leaders, most of the historic Protestant churches as communities expressed their support for the civil rights movement. Many leaders spoke out for civil rights, and white, southern churchwomen began quietly building networks of relationships with African American women even while their husbands were proclaiming that segregation was a permanent fixture of southern life. Some leaders of fundamentalist churches, meanwhile, acknowledged that their own churches had failed to take a positive stance toward civil rights, for example, in Carl F. H. Henry's *The Uneasy Conscience of Modern Fundamentalism* (1947).

Despite the social and political conservatism of some of their church leaders, most of the historic Protestant churches as communities expressed their support for the civil rights movement.

The movement to include gay and lesbian people fully in the life of our churches today can be seen as a parallel socially progressive movement. True to our history, many of those who support progressive attitudes toward gay and lesbian people espouse very traditional theological views and attitudes toward Christian worship. Gay students I have taught through my career tend to be deeply spiritual and aspiring to Christlike holiness. Many of them espouse traditional theology and attitudes toward Christian worship. We need to remember this in the bitterness that often accompanies debates over these issues in our churches and lay aside conspiracy theories that claim that simply including homosexual people in the life of the church amounts to a capitulation to secular culture or to liberal theological views. That's just not the way it is.

The legacy of Christian progressive social action is grounded in the gospel. God became a human for our sake in Jesus Christ. Christianity cannot be concerned about spiritual matters only. We're concerned about the material world because it is God's good creation and it is the world in which God became incarnate in Jesus Christ.

Legacy Three: Our Conservatisms

Progressive Protestants often hold theologically conservative ideas while they espouse politically and socially progressive activism. But conservatism is a many-splendored thing, and among the legacies of historic Protestant churches are distinct forms of conservatism that have been long-standing parts of the Christian cultures of our churches. These too are legacies we should treasure and by which we should be encouraged. I do not just mean the conservatism expressed in our historic creeds, confessions, and liturgies. I'll say more on those in the next chapter. Back up a few more decades: I mean particular conservative cultures that contrasted sharply in the mid-1800s: an evangelical form of Protestant conservatism and a high-church form of Protestant conservatism.

One form of conservatism can be described as the evangelical pattern, notable from the time of the First Great Awakening from the 1720s in the British North American colonies. The First Great Awakening and subsequent religious revivals called for heartfelt repentance and faith in Christ on the part of Christian people, and it witnessed revivals among Anglicans, Congregationalists, Presbyterians, and Dutch Reformed, with Methodists and Baptists increasingly involved in revivals as the Awakening proceeded.

By the late 1700s and early 1800s, when the movement morphed into what has been called the Second Great Awakening, evangelists took up such new techniques as using extended "camp meetings" following a pattern set by Scots-Irish Presbyterian communion celebrations. They also developed a kit of evangelistic techniques such as the evangelistic "altar call" at the conclusion of services. At about the same time, Pietistic expressions of Lutheranism and of Reformed faith advocated similarly emotive, if less spectacular, expressions of faith in the United States and Canada.

Although the Second Great Awakening affected many Protestant groups, it also provoked reactions in the early 1800s in other Protestant communities. What these forms of reaction had in common was a suspicion that revivalistic preachers had reduced Christianity to emotional experiences and had failed to emphasize the historic and objective forms of Christian faith. These reactions offered a second pattern of conservatism beside the evangelical pattern. There were three prominent expressions of reaction against revivalistic religion in the early 1800s.

- German Reformed and Presbyterian theologians associated with the Mercersburg School of Theology in Pennsylvania advocated commitment to traditional creeds and confessions common to Christian churches, and more traditional or liturgical forms of worship.
- Many Episcopalians in the United States were influenced by the Oxford or Tractarian Movement that developed in the Church of England in the 1830s and spread to North America within that decade. The Oxford Movement emphasized the continuity of Anglicanism with the medieval Catholic Church in England, and this appeared outwardly in their emphasis on liturgical seasons, clerical vestments, and ritual actions in worship.
- Lutheran theologians in the same period began to emphasize Luther's own continuities with Catholicism, his litur-

> gical practices, and the centrality of the Lord's Supper in Lutheranism. One particular group of Prussian Lutherans who strongly upheld their Lutheran identity and objected to being forced into a union with Reformed churches left Prussia and came to America. Disembarking in St. Louis, they formed a distinctive Lutheran body that came to be called the Lutheran Church, Missouri Synod (LCMS).

The combination of the Second Great Awakening with these early nineteenth-century catholicizing and confessional conservative movements gave most American Protestant (and Anglican) groups two distinctive parties within their churches: a revivalistic or pietistic party, and a high-church, liturgically oriented party. These vied with each other in a More Conservative Than Thou competition internal to each denominational group. Almost all of the historic Protestant churches in the United States continue to reflect these distinctive forms of conservatism.

For example, although Methodist societies were strongly evangelical at the beginning of the 1800s, they developed their own version of high-church teachings by the end of that century, sometimes arguing that John Wesley was himself a "high-church" Anglican. The African Methodist Episcopal (AME) bishop Henry McNeal Turner advocated revived use of John Wesley's revision of *The Book of Common Prayer.* In response to Anglican beliefs about the "apostolic succession" of bishops, Turner elaborated a belief in the "presbyteral succession" of Methodist clergy. As a result of his reforms, many historic, urban AME churches today reflect rather pure forms of eighteenth-century Anglican worship, including the chanting of the commandments as preface to the communion ritual.

Another distinctive pattern of Protestant theological conservatism developed from the time between the World Wars in the twentieth century when historic Protestant churches in the United States were influenced by Neo-Orthodoxy. Associated with the Swiss theologian Karl Barth (1886–1968), Neo-Orthodoxy represented a movement away from the theologically liberal form of progressivism that prevailed after the turn of the twentieth century. Disillusioned by the terrors of World War I, including terrors enabled by modern technologies, Barth himself began to seek a more scriptural and doctrinally responsible foundation for Christian faith. He did not, however, accept contemporary versions of Protestant fundamentalism either, affirming the use of modern biblical scholarship and active engagement with critical contemporary issues.

For old-line churches in the United States, Neo-Orthodoxy had strong resonances with the older high-church form of conservatism in theology and liturgy coupled with the postmillennial emphasis on progressive social activism.

Barth and Neo-Orthodox theologians following him engaged themselves in concrete, socially and politically progressive movements, most notably, the "Confessing Church" movement that stood against Nazism in German states. For old-line churches in the United States, Neo-Orthodoxy had strong resonances with the older high-church form of conservatism in theology and liturgy coupled with the postmillennial emphasis on progressive social activism. That was not an unprecedented combination in American churches.

Legacy Four: Roots beyond America

The historic Protestant churches of the United States grew out of Christian traditions inherited from Europe, and in particular, from the period of sixteenth-century reformations in European Christianity. Historians today are reluctant to speak only of the *Protestant* Reformation because we recognize a variety of reforming movements in the 1500s, including

- Catholic reforms;
- the Lutheran reforming movement that led to the formation of a number of independent regional churches in the 1500s;
- the Reformed tradition associated with Zwingli and Calvin that led to separate churches in some German states, Holland, France, and Scotland, including Congregational and Presbyterian churches as well as groups that have the word Reformed in their names;
- widely differing modes of reform in England in that century culminating in the establishment of the Church of England in the reign of Elizabeth I in the late 1500s; and
- reforming movements that we often group together as "Anabaptist" or a "Radical" Reformation.

Historic Protestant churches in the United States have particular ties to the reforming movements of Britain and Ireland where

Protestant churches were divided according to forms of church government or polity.

- The episcopal form of church governance, which gave a strong role to bishops (*episcopi*), characterized the Church of England and the Episcopal Church of Scotland. These would give rise to the Episcopal Church and to Methodist churches in the United States.
- The presbyterian form of church governance did not utilize bishops and gave a strong role to gatherings of church elders (*presbyteri*) called presbyteries. This form of governance characterized the Church of Scotland and Presbyterian churches in England and in the United States.
- The congregational form of governance gave the strongest role to the local congregation and characterized Congregational churches in the British Isles and in the United States. Baptist churches typically conformed to the congregational form of governance, and many Baptist churches were simply Congregational congregations that had voted not to baptize infants.

In 1689 the United Kingdom had enacted an Act of Toleration that allowed for the public worship of dissenting Protestant churches apart from the Church of England and the Church of Scotland. By that time, tolerated British churches included the Episcopal Church of Scotland, Presbyterian and Congregational churches, Baptist churches, and Quaker meetings. The Act of Toleration applied in the North American colonies in addition to the distinctive forms of toleration that had been granted in provincial charters.

These forms of British Christianity dominated the religious life of the early American colonies. But other forms of Christian faith were planted here as well. The Quaker colony of Pennsylvania allowed a high degree of religious toleration that encouraged German-speaking groups to settle there, including not only Lutherans and German Reformed, but German-speaking Anabaptist groups and Moravians as well. New York and New Jersey had settlements of Dutch colonists who established Dutch Reformed churches. The Maryland colony had an unusual provision that allowed the formal toleration of Catholicism.

The older Protestant churches connected American churches to their roots beyond the European reformations of the 1500s. It's important to remember that Presbyterian congregations in Scotland worship in the same medieval stone church buildings where their Catholic ancestors worshipped in the Middle Ages. The same is true of Lutheran churches in Germany and Scandinavian countries, and of Anglican churches in England and Wales and in much of Ireland. People in these churches sense a connection to the past in a way that Christians in the United States can scarcely envision.

The Legacy of All Legacies: The Gospel

The great legacy that our churches share with other Christians is the legacy of the gospel, proclaimed in the New Testament scriptures, affirmed in our historic creeds, enacted in the sacraments, and celebrated annually in the pattern of the Christian year from Advent to Christmas to Epiphany to Lent and to Easter. Martin Luther wrote in his *Ninety-Five Theses* that

The great treasure of the church
is the gospel of the grace and glory of God.

What do our churches really hold in common? What do our churches hold to be the center of our faith? We begin and end with the gospel, "the great treasure of the church." Let's punctuate our quest for encouragement, then, with a single story that we profess together as churches. It's not the story about Martin Luther or John Calvin or Good Queen Bess or the Mayflower Pilgrims or John Wesley. It is not about abortion or homosexuality. It's the gospel. In the words of an old song I learned in my childhood, it's "the old, old story of Jesus and his love." The gospel gives us confidence.

What do our churches really hold in common? What do our churches hold to be the center of our faith? We begin and end with the gospel, "the great treasure of the church."

The gospel is not a boring generalization like, "God is nice and we ought to be nice too." There's nothing wrong with being nice, but the gospel is not about niceness. It's a very, very specific story. According to St. Paul, in some of the earliest words written down about Jesus, the gospel goes like this: "Now I would remind you [plural], brothers and sisters, of the good news [gospel] that I proclaimed to you.... For I handed on to you as of first importance what I in turn had received: that Christ died for our sins in accordance with the scriptures, and that he was buried, and that he was raised on the third day in accordance with the scriptures" (1 Cor 15:1, 3-4 NRSV).

The gospel has to do with the life, death, and resurrection of Jesus Christ. Our churches have historically recited the gospel in the words of the ancient Western baptismal affirmation that we call the Apostles' Creed. Here's a good word: "[I believe] in Jesus Christ his only Son our Lord, who was conceived by the Holy Spirit, born of the Virgin Mary, suffered under Pontius Pilate, was crucified, died and was buried. He descended to the dead. On the third day he rose again."

The ecumenical movement has emphasized the importance of the Nicene Creed as the most widely affirmed Christian profession of faith. The Episcopal Church and historic Lutheran churches have used the Nicene Creed since the time of their origins as distinct groups in the 1500s. Although Methodists and Presbyterians did not as regularly utilize the Nicene Creed, they came to do so in the twentieth century as a result of their ecumenical contacts and commitments.

The Nicene Creed echoes even more directly the words of the primitive Christian gospel in 1 Corinthians 15: "[We believe] in one Lord, Jesus Christ,...For us and for our salvation he came down from heaven, was incarnate of the Holy Spirit and the Virgin Mary and became truly human. For our sake he was crucified under Pontius Pilate; he suffered death and was buried. On the third day he rose again in accordance with the Scriptures."

What is common to all of these historic creeds is the simple narrative of the work of God in Jesus Christ. The gospel is at the heart of our historic creeds and confessions of faith.

We celebrate the gospel every Sunday as we remember the day of the resurrection. We celebrate the gospel every year as we remember the prophecies of Christ (Advent), the birth of Jesus Christ (Christmas), the revelation of Christ to the world (Epiphany), Christ's suffering and eventual death as a human being (Lent), and Christ's resurrection from the dead (Easter). We proclaim the gospel in the Supper of the Lord and in the rite of baptism. The gospel is "the ground of our hope," the foundation for everything else we do, the heart of it all. Here's a good word:

Christ has died.
Christ is risen.
Christ will come again.

beep *beep* *beep* *beep*

Chapter Four

STRENGTHS

I have tried to expose some of the more pernicious myths about our churches. The last chapter explored the strengths that lie in our traditions, our legacies as Christians. But what might be the continuing, present, and newly renewed strengths of America's older Protestant churches?

Chapter 2 has shown that, contrary to the stereotypes, America's older Protestant churches continue to have a strong core of committed, active church members. Although it is true that weekly church attendance as well as overall membership in American churches of all sorts have been declining consistently for decades, there is evidence that membership declines in historic Protestant churches are overwhelmingly of inactive members, and some of the decline in weekly worship attendance reflects the contemporary situation that active families do not consistently worship weekly as active members did earlier in the twentieth century.

There are some contemporary strengths of old-line churches that ought to be celebrated today.

Some of the great strengths of historic Protestant churches lie in the legacies that we bring from the past into the present. Preeminent among these legacies is the narrative of the gospel, the central message of God's work on our behalf in Christ's life, death, and resurrection. But there are some contemporary strengths of oldline churches that ought to be celebrated today. In particular, I'll hold up a) renewed traditions of doctrine and liturgy, b) renewed forms of Christian music, c) stronger expectations for the Christian formation of adult believers, d) institutions for multigenerational transmission of church cultures, and e) church-based benevolent institutions.

Doctrine and Liturgy

One of the strengths of our churches is the inheritance and contemporary expression of Christian doctrine and liturgy. These are not only legacies inherited from the past but also strengths that reflect contemporary developments and contemporary consensus in our churches, and they enable us to transmit a core of church cultures across generations.

Our churches have doctrinal statements typically inherited from the age of the Reformations, for example, Articles of Religion for Episcopalians and Methodists, the Augsburg Confession for Lutherans, and the Westminster Confession of Faith for Reformed Christians. They also have forms of Christian teaching—catechisms—that reflect a similar heritage, for example, the Catechism of *The Book of Common Prayer*, the Luther Small Catechism, and the Westminster Shorter Catechism. Individual church members are not strictly bound by these denominational statements: the doctrinal statements express what communities (denominations and congregations) believe as communities. Even when church members are asked to memorize a historic catechism like the Luther Small Catechism, they are not asked to subscribe personally to it. They are asked if they *know* the teachings of their churches, but the doctrine they profess solemnly at baptism or confirmation is almost universally in the words of the ancient Western Christian baptismal profession we call the Apostles' Creed. That is to say, they *profess* common Christian teachings and they also *know* the particular teachings of their own churches.

Clergy in these churches are typically asked at the time of ordination if they will teach the doctrines of their church. It's understood that they have the freedom to express their own opinions so long as they faithfully explicate the scriptures and correctly state the teachings of their churches *as* the teachings of the churches. There are legends about Episcopal priests with thirty-nine buttons on their cassocks who regularly leave specific buttons unfastened, suggesting their objection to specific articles in the Thirty-Nine Articles of Religion. In this case, though, it's not about their liberalism; it's a question of More Conservative Than Thou: their objections tend to be from the conservative Anglo-Catholic side directed against the more flagrantly Protestant-leaning Articles. I have heard rumors that some ~~atrociously wicked~~ clergy in historic Protestant churches *only* state their own opinions and not the teachings of their churches. If that's the case, then they're not doing their job and they're not keeping their commitments to teach the doctrines of their churches. And, it seems to me, they're dissing the work of the Holy Spirit in the history of our communities and in contemporary corporate expressions of Christian teachings and practices. But they do have a degree of freedom so long as they remain responsible to their commitments to teach the doctrines of their churches.

Doctrinal statements in historic Protestant churches have not remained entirely static since the time of the Reformations. Perhaps Lutheran churches have remained most staunch in resisting the temptation to alter doctrinal statements or add new ones. In the most recent revision of *The Book of Common Prayer*, the Episcopal Church added the Definition of Faith of the Council of Chalcedon and the Chicago-Lambeth Quadrilateral alongside the Articles of Religion. The United Methodist Church has a more contemporary statement of "Our Theological Task," adopted in 1972 and revised in 1988, reflecting ecumenical consensus in some areas. A doctrinal resolution adopted by The UMC in 1972 and reaffirmed since that time states that the anti-Catholic material in its Articles of Religion should be understood as directed against specific late-medieval Catholic teachings and practices, not necessarily against the contemporary teachings and practices of the Catholic Church. The Presbyterian Church (U.S.A.) has added "A Brief Statement of Faith" following older and more historic Reformed confessions in its *Book of Confessions*. Moreover, it has added some contemporary annotations to the Westminster Confession in a "Declaratory Statement" that explains that the teaching about divine predestination must be "held in harmony with the doctrine of [God's] love to all mankind, his gift of his Son to be the propitiation for the sins of the whole world, and his readiness to bestow his saving grace on all who seek it."

Historic Protestant churches,* as churches, *have remained rather consistent in affirming historic Christian teachings.

Despite the fact that these additions, contemporary statements, clarifications, and annotations were added in the twentieth century, the truth is that they are not particularly liberal. Historic Protestant churches, *as churches,* have remained rather consistent in affirming historic Christian teachings. Breaking News Flash: Protestant Churches Haven't Changed Their Beliefs. On the same page with Generalísimo Francisco Franco Is Still Dead. No, that doesn't have the level of conflict it takes to make contemporary news, which consistently favors stories about this or that pastor's or bishop's ~~heretical~~ eccentric, individual beliefs or despicable behaviors. Man bites dog; pastor preaches heresy; and so on.

Historic forms of worship also transmit traditional beliefs in our churches. As with doctrine, most of the historic Protestant churches have inherited forms of worship from their European forebears. For Anglicans, including Episcopalians, this inheritance was transmitted through *The Book of Common Prayer.* The traditional words of the Prayer Book are well known in the English-speaking world:

> Dearly beloved, we are gathered together here in the sight of God, and in the face of this congregation, to join together this man and this woman in holy matrimony...

> Ye that do truly and earnestly repent you of your sins, and are in love and charity with your neighbors, and intend to lead a

> new life, following the commandments of God, and walking from henceforth in his holy ways...

Methodist churches, including the AME, AME Zion, CME, and UMC, inherited very much the same words from their Anglican roots. Lutheran and Presbyterian communities also had older liturgies derived from their church traditions beyond the United States, and in English-speaking contexts, Lutherans have sometimes appropriated the ritual words of *The Book of Common Prayer.*

From the 1960s, historic Protestant churches engaged in a process of liturgical revision—revision of our shared worship patterns—along with leaders and scholars of the Catholic Church. The result has been revised liturgies using more contemporary language and reflecting ancient Christian traditions of worship that had been little known and little studied earlier. These revised liturgies bear similarities in language—often the very same words—and structural parallels across traditions. We can now attend worship across our traditions and largely know the content of the services that will be used. That even applies to Protestants attending Catholic masses and *vice versa* since the 1970s, even if we do not yet share full, visible communion (fellowship) with each other.

Some of the results of these liturgical revisions are as follows:

- The use of a consistently Trinitarian and creedal pattern for the eucharistic prayer, the central prayer of thanksgiving in the celebration of the Lord's Supper
- The use of congregational responses to each of the three parts of the eucharistic prayer, including the following congregational acclamation—originally developed in English-

language Catholic revisions of the mass in the 1970s—that concludes the second section of the prayer, the section offering thanks for the work of God in Jesus Christ:

Christ has died.
Christ is risen.
Christ will come again.

- The use of an interrogative pattern of affirmation for those who come to be baptized or to profess their faith in confirmation following the ancient pattern described in Latin versions of a text called *The Apostolic Tradition*
- The renewed use of renunciations of evil in the rites of baptism and confirmation

As with doctrine, the revisions of liturgies in the twentieth century do not reflect a liberal outlook except perhaps in the use of more contemporary language in contrast to the "thee-thou" language of older rituals.

As with doctrine, the revisions of liturgies in the twentieth century do not reflect a liberal outlook except perhaps in the use of more contemporary language in contrast to the "thee-thou" language of older rituals. It would be fair to say that they have a "conserving" or even conservative character, reflecting a renewed inheritance of ancient Christian worship patterns studied in the last century.

Music

Along with the inheritance of doctrine and patterns of worship is a rich inheritance of Christian music in historic Protestant churches. *The Bay Psalm Book* (1640) was the first book printed in the British colonies of North America, and it reflected the Reformed (Congregational and Presbyterian) tradition of singing the Psalms in "meter," that is, in English verse. Lutheran and Anglican churches brought their own traditions of chanting and hymnody to America. When Methodists showed up from the 1760s, they brought the hymns of Charles Wesley edited by his brother John.

Although these older musical traditions may appear very traditional in comparison with Contemporary Christian music, there has been a long and ongoing process of revision of songs. Most of the Charles Wesley hymns that we sing today, for example, are set to tunes that date from the 1800s or even the 1900s. The coupling of John Newton's eighteenth-century words "Amazing grace, how sweet the sound!" with the folk tune "New Britain" to which we almost always sing these words, was a nineteenth-century development.

We've had a living, vigorous tradition of church music that extends right into the use of "Contemporary Christian" music and musical traditions reflecting particular cultural and ethnic traditions today, and in fact our musical traditions have been interacting with popular music for centuries. In the early 1800s, Methodists and Baptists and Presbyterians all began to utilize spirituals and folk songs marketed in the United States in collections like *The Sacred Harp* (1844), the first book to have the tune for "New Britain" used to sing "Amazing Grace." Eventually, songs like this would become part of the inheritance of almost all Christian communities. Similarly, in the late 1800s, some Protestant groups began to devise performance spaces like Victorian music halls and to cultivate Christian music patterned after the popular music heard in such venues. That's what we call Gospel music today. Resisted at first, a small canon of Gospel songs became part of a common Christian inheritance of music from the late 1800s and the early 1900s in African American as well as Euro-American churches.

The advent of Christian folk music and Contemporary Christian music in the 1960s and '70s continued these trajectories of utilizing contemporary musical genres to express Christian convictions. It might be worth noting that when the *Sacred Harp* songs and spirituals and Gospel songs originated, they were not at first performed in Sunday-morning worship settings. They were sung originally in informal settings or in assemblies designed to attract non-churchgoing folks. Only later did some select examples of these musical genres find their way into more traditional worship settings. These genres—spirituals, Gospel, Contemporary Christian—have been joined in recent years by musical genres reflecting particular cultural traditions, such as musical traditions characteristic of Central and South America or of Asian and African cultures.

What's really happening, then, is a cautious, contemporary appropriation, evaluation, and reinvention of musical traditions in historic Protestant churches as well as newer evangelical communities in the United States.

What's really happening, then, is a cautious, contemporary appropriation, evaluation, and reinvention of musical traditions in historic Protestant churches as well as newer evangelical communities in the United States. What's also happening is an ongoing process of marketing on the part of independent music corporations that sometimes stand in tension with traditional forms of worship in historic churches. But the process of evaluation and utilization of newer musical genres continues a tradition of musical innovation that remains one of the great strengths of old-line churches in the United States.

Strong Expectations for the Christian Formation of Adult Church Members

One of the stereotypes about older Protestant churches characterizes them as doctrinally and morally lax, with low expectations for serious Christian formation. The old adage "Where there's smoke, there's fire" really does apply here. There's a reason why our churches won this reputation. Some of us worked really hard at it. But the counterintuitive fact is that older Protestant churches today have higher expectations for church membership than they had forty years ago. I see your suspicious looks out there. Stick with me.

Let me begin by giving you the example with which I am most familiar, namely, The United Methodist Church and its predecessors. Warning: what I say about United Methodists here is probably far more drastic than what has happened with other churches, but that's why The UMC provides a good illustration.

At the beginning of the twentieth century, three predecessor denominations of The United Methodist Church (Methodist Episcopal

Church; Methodist Episcopal Church, South; and Methodist Protestant Church) had only one ~~pitifully wimpy~~ doctrinal question for church membership:

> Do you profess the Christian faith as contained in the scriptures of the New Testament?

Now really, almost anyone could answer that positively. Some Very Traditional Methodist people pointed out at mid-century that Methodists (this is pre–United Methodist) did have an Article of Religion asserting that the Old and New Testaments are not contradictory to each other. So the question was revised to ask:

> Do you profess the Christian faith as contained in the scriptures of the Old and New Testaments?

Still, though, it was a near-total wimp-out, with almost no specific content. In recent decades, The United Methodist Church has revised its services for Baptism and Christian profession of faith (confirmation) following Catholic as well as Anglican and Protestant traditions. The UMC now asks:

> Do you believe in God the Father?
> Do you believe in Jesus Christ?
> Do you believe in the Holy Spirit?

Candidates do not simply respond "Yea" or "Sure" or "You betcha" or just nod their heads in response to these questions. They are expected to repeat out loud, in response to each question, the article of the Apostles' Creed on each point. And The UMC asks questions like these that they did not ask in the past:

> Do you renounce the spiritual forces of wickedness, reject the evil powers of this world, and repent of your sin?
> Do you accept the freedom and power God gives you to resist evil, injustice, and oppression in whatever forms they present themselves?
> Do you confess Jesus Christ as your Savior, put your whole trust in his grace, and promise to serve him as your Lord, in union with the church which Christ has opened to people of all ages, nations, and races?

These are serious questions, so don't miss the point here. The period when Methodists were asking that ~~silly~~ ~~wimpy~~ ~~low-down good-for-nothing~~ weak question, "Do you profess the Christian faith as contained in the scriptures of the Old and New Testaments?" was the same period in which Methodists developed a bloated, inactive church membership. Anybody out there think that was a complete coincidence? Wake up. At the same time, pastors collected all the names on the church rolls they could possibly collect, whether the folks named had any intentions of being Christians; they baptized with as little water as possible, sometimes using ~~cutesy~~ ~~stupid~~ little roses to dip in the water; and membership in adult Sunday school classes declined precipitously. It was easy religion. It was ~~an abomination~~ a disaster. Christ, have mercy upon us. Maybe there really *was* a reason why Jon Stewart had the impression that Methodism is (or at least *was*) "like the University of Phoenix of religion." But that era in Methodist life was well before the University of Phoenix arose.

Maybe Methodists were the worst. Really I don't know, but I'm willing to take it on. We were pretty bad. I remember the essentials of Methodism at one point boiled down to, "You can believe anything you want and you can drink beer." I seriously doubt that

Episcopalians or Lutherans in this period had questions as easy as the one Methodists had. But I can see why a Methodist like Dean M. Kelley placed so much emphasis in 1972 on weak membership expectations.

Not only have we asked tougher questions of members since the 1970s and 1980s, our churches have been involved in large-scale programs for deeper Christian formation in recent decades.

Not only have we asked tougher questions of members since the 1970s and 1980s, our churches have been involved in large-scale programs for deeper Christian formation in recent decades. The Disciple Bible study series produced by The United Methodist Publishing House and utilized widely in older Protestant churches, offers an extensive immersion in the scriptures, with weekly expectations of reading, prayer, and commitment. I am not making this up: two million people have now gone through the Disciple series, and new studies like Covenant Bible Study continue to bring deep formation through scripture study to old-line Protestant churches. Other programs like Cursillo or Emmaus Walks or programs of spiritual direction have brought participants into deeper Christian spiritual formation than was available forty years ago.

So I want to make the case, despite all the ~~bellyaching griping~~ stereotypes, that our churches have a stronger membership today, better formed in Christian scriptures and Christian spiritual traditions, professing the faith publicly in a much more specific and dramatic way than we did fifty years ago. If that doesn't answer to popular stereotypes of older Protestant churches in the United States, then maybe the stereotypes themselves need to be ~~consigned to the flames of hell~~ seriously questioned.

Institutions for Multigenerational Transmission of Cultures

One of the strengths of older Christian communities in the United States—and here I could include Catholic as well as older Anglican and Protestant communities in this—is a web of institutions designed to transmit cultures across generations. Colleges, universities, theological schools, lay training institutes, permanent encampments, retreat centers, and a host of other institutions serve the purpose of transmitting our ways of being Christian to future generations.

Compare these institutions of historic churches to newer, independent Christian congregations such as megachurches that have not yet faced the critical moment of a transition in pastoral leadership. Megachurches have demonstrated that they can attract significant numbers of people for a space of decades during the leadership of a charismatic, founding pastor. They have not *yet* demonstrated that they can transmit Christian cultures beyond that first generation of leadership. Consider Robert Schuller's Crystal Cathedral in Orange County, California, an institution that faced its first transition in pastoral leadership when Schuller stepped down. The congregation filed for bankruptcy in 2010, and ended up selling its magnificent campus to the Catholic Diocese of Orange. I think it's fair to say that this congregation did not succeed in transmitting its culture to new generations. Some of the megachurches will succeed in doing that, and I venture to say that they will begin to look a lot more like America's historic Protestant churches when they do because—boring as this may seem—they will have developed institutions for the multigenerational transmission of church cultures.

I hasten to say that not all church institutions take the transmission of church cultures as their primary goal. Most church-based educational institutions, at least among Protestant and Anglican churches, are privately chartered institutions governed by their own boards of directors. They have complicated ways of interfacing with churches. Duke University, for example, is a private, self-governing institution whose charter specifies that a third of its trustees are elected by the North Carolina Annual Conference of The United Methodist Church, a third of its trustees are elected by the Western North Carolina Annual Conference of The United Methodist Church, and a third of its trustees are elected by the university's alumni. The university is accredited by the University Senate of The United Methodist Church, but beyond these ties, Duke University sets its own course. Parallel situations exist for other institutions of higher learning founded by older Protestant groups in the United States.

But within institutions like this, there is typically a core group that serves as a more intense focus of relationship with churches. At Duke University, the Divinity School and Duke Chapel serve to connect the university to the life of churches, including The United Methodist Church. At smaller liberal arts colleges, the office of the chaplain and perhaps a department of religious studies may serve a similar function, keeping a more explicit tie to sponsoring churches.

Denominationally related colleges, universities, and theological schools have served not only to recruit generations of church leaders but also to form generations of laypersons with strong ties to our traditions of Christian formation.

Colleges, universities, and theological schools like these have served not only to recruit generations of church leaders but also to form generations of laypersons with strong ties to our traditions of Christian formation. Consider Lon Morris College, the little Methodist junior college I attended. My parents went to church summer camps there in the early 1940s. My wife's parents met there in the late 1940s, and her father, who had grown up in a different denomination, became a Methodist there. My wife and I met there in the early 1970s, and the school really could be described as a Methodist breeding ground. For which we are grateful. Our daughter graduated from the college in 2003. Although the college did not enforce chapel attendance or impose any religious tests on its faculty, it formed generations of leaders for its sponsoring church and very few students in the college could have missed the influence the church had on it.

Institutions like this face all kinds of contemporary problems. The fact that they are independently chartered and do not typically impose denominational tests on faculty or staff members means that denominational ties (Christian ties) can loosen through a period of decades. Many formerly church-related institutions have cut their ties to church bodies. Vanderbilt University, Syracuse University, Northwestern University, and the University of Southern California, just to name a few, were all related to Methodist denominations at one time. All of them subsequently cut ties to churches. The fact that they're independently chartered gave their trustees the option of doing this, though if we consider the churches' long involvement in these schools as an investment, the churches ended up with little to show for their years of support for the institutions beyond a venue for social service by education. There's nothing wrong with social service by education, but the founding churches intended that they would serve to transmit church cultures.

Other schools find it simply difficult to survive even if they cultivate ties to churches. The little Methodist college I described above closed its doors in the summer of 2012 after more than 140 years of service in East Texas, the oldest two-year college west of the Mississippi. The church tried for decades to support the college; in the end, it didn't work. God bless the memory of Lon Morris College, "ever worthy of our homage," as we sang. I preached at a service to remember and commemorate the college, and I asked, "If not by Lon Morris College, how will we transmit a rich, Christian culture across generations?"

Educational institutions are only one instance of church-related structures by which church cultures can be transmitted to new generations. Other institutions such as church-related retreat centers and encampments tend to remain much more focused on their work related to sponsoring church groups, and they also serve as venues to transmit church cultures across generations. Many of these institutions are also independently chartered, but their missions tend to be much more focused on work such as spiritual formation that is directly related to the religious life of Christian communities. Anyone involved in ministries like these can tell you that there's fairly intense competition among them, and it isn't easy for them (as with smaller educational institutions) to forge workable business plans and budgets that will enable their persistence into the future.

Perhaps most important among the church-related institutions that transmit church cultures are the publishing enterprises that each of the denominations has fostered.

Perhaps most important among the church-related institutions that transmit church cultures are the publishing enterprises that each of the denominations has fostered. Church-related publishing houses have not only published such official church materials as hymnals, catechisms, books of worship, and Sunday school literature; they've increasingly sponsored newer and more creative ways of forming people as Christians. In the 1980s, The United Methodist Publishing House instituted four series of DISCIPLE Bible studies. These involved an intensive study of the whole Bible, and require participants to commit themselves to daily Bible reading, prayer, and participation in weekly sessions. To date, more than two million people have participated in the DISCIPLE Bible study series. That's more than a quarter of the entire US membership of The UMC, although the

DISCIPLE series is used widely outside of United Methodist Church circles. Church-related publishing houses have faced immense challenges with the advent of new media for publication in recent decades and vigorous competition from mass-marketing media outlets. As with other church-related institutions, the trend in denominational life has been to shift funding to local programs rather than national or international-level denominational programs, further weakening centrally organized publishing and marketing efforts.

Institutions in general are not easily maintained across longer spans of time. We need to tend them carefully, recognizing their distinctive characters, and continuing to ask how they serve the churches. But we need them if we want our ministries and our traditions of Christian life to be transmitted to future generations.

Benevolent Infrastructures

When the Boston Marathon bombings occurred on April 15, 2013, most of the surviving victims and one of the perpetrators were taken to the Beth Israel Deaconess Hospital. You might guess that the "Beth Israel" part of that hospital's name reflects its Jewish benevolent heritage. The word *Deaconess* reflects the hospital's heritage in the inner-city mission work of the Methodist Episcopal Church in the late 1800s and the early 1900s—in fact, the deaconess movement that Lucy Rider Meyer had pioneered in Chicago. It's just one of the thousands of institutions that have grown out of the missions of older churches to serve others following the example and teachings of Jesus Christ.

In addition to institutions that serve to transmit church cultures across generations described in the previous section, older Protestant churches have developed a complex nexus of benevolent institutions in the United States and in fact throughout the world. We do not have to "reinvent the wheel" when it comes to serving others. But it is also a challenge: maintaining benevolent institutions across generations, and maintaining their explicit ties to church bodies, proves to be more difficult than one might imagine.

Church-related benevolent institutions have been able to forge alliances between themselves and across denominational boundaries to further their work.

On the positive side, our church-related benevolent institutions have been able to forge alliances between themselves and across denominational boundaries to further their work. Church World Service (CWS) is a collaborative organization born in 1947 in the aftermath of World War II that today provides basic support (food, water, clothing, shelter) for those in need. CWS sponsors annual CROP walks (Christian Rural Overseas Program) to combat hunger. Historic Protestant churches in the United States form the backbone of Church World Service, though a number of other denominations also participate in the work of CWS. But CWS is just one example of collaborative work. The Life and Work movement was a constitutive part of the early ecumenical movement that sought unity in church outreach efforts. One of their slogans was, "Doctrine divides; service unites." All of our churches participate in ecumenical ventures inspired by the Life and Work movement.

Our benevolent institutions have proven highly effective. It's worth asking if they actually provide infrastructures for the missionary work of other Protestant denominations, and here I mean conservative evangelical groups. If the Assemblies of God, for example, start a mission to Zimbabwe, my impression is that they don't have to worry about founding hospitals or schools, because existing Christian hospitals and schools are available both through the Catholic Church and historic Protestant churches. They can rely on those existing benevolent institutions and focus their own resources and efforts on their evangelistic work. A lot of our resources, by contrast, go to the upkeep of institutions like schools and hospitals. Are we underwriting the evangelistic efforts of other churches through our benevolent institutions? What if they had no existing educational or medical institutions in missionary locations?

Our benevolent institutions have proven highly effective. It's worth asking if they actually provide infrastructures for the missionary work of other Protestant denominations, and here I mean conservative evangelical groups.

Mentioning educational institutions in this context raises another question. Do our educational institutions exist to transmit our church cultures, as discussed in the previous section, or do they exist solely as a benevolent service to broader communities? The answer, really, is both. There's nothing wrong with sponsoring educational institutions as a service to the broader community, and many church-sponsored educational institutions have in fact defined their missions in the latter way. In his novel *Cryptonomicon* (1999), Neal Stephenson describes the following supposedly fictitious situation: "The town in question sports three small colleges: one founded by the State of California and two founded by Protestant denominations that are now actively reviled by the majority of their faculty." Completely fictitious? I doubt it.

When educational institutions begin to understand themselves as benevolent foundations for community good rather than providing a locus for transmitting a specific church culture, they're on a slippery slope that leads many of them eventually to dissolve ties with their founding churches. "Thank you very much, we'll take the property and the endowments and gratefully remember the founding denomination in wistful comments in founders'-day speeches. If at all."

This is really a problem faced by benevolent institutions in general. Benevolence was once an almost exclusive enterprise of religious groups. In the early twentieth century, benevolence was increasingly professionalized, and many church groups came to believe that supporting professional benevolent organizations would be more effective than working through explicitly church-related groups. The problem this raised, however, was that church members became less directly involved in benevolent work and were simply encouraged to send donations to professional organizations. This trend exacerbated the problems of trying to keep organizations related to the churches.

In recent decades there has been a trend toward more direct involvement in benevolent work on the part of local congregations and church members. This has led many congregations to form independent 501(c)(3) corporations for their charitable work. These corporations have the advantage of direct contact with charitable work. They can also detract from centralized efforts that can deal with broader, systemic issues like the underlying causes of disease and poverty, often in collaboration with ecumenical partners. In the long term, we see a cycle of more localized efforts and more systemic charitable work, and we need both. The broader network of charitable institutions is itself a gift that historic Protestant churches have fostered. It reflects our consistent efforts to see the good reign of God become a reality in our world.

Chapter Five

FUTURE

So continue encouraging each other and building each other up, just like you are doing already.

1 Thessalonians 5:11

So what do we do? We've identified some of the myths, realities, legacies, and strengths of our churches. None of this masks the fact that genuine problems face America's historic Protestant churches. Some of these problems are very real; some of them are problems of appearance and representation, but those are no less problems. We shouldn't let others define who we are.

In what follows, I offer some thoughts on practices that will edify or build up our churches. You should harbor the appropriate suspicion that I am a historian, and not any kind of expert on the practical life of churches. But history often has insights for contemporary practice. What follows are some insights on edifying practices that arise from our history and the contemporary situations considered here.

Strengthen the Core

It might seem counterintuitive that the first thing I would say about facing the future is that we need to tend, first of all, to strengthening the core of our existing constituencies. But healthy organisms grow. I have suggested in the previous chapter that historic Protestant churches in the United States have made considerable strides toward strengthening core constituencies through more stringent requirements for Christian profession and church membership and through stronger educational and formational programs than we have had in the past. But it's no time to stop this work. Continue to strengthen the core membership. A strong core of membership will be the basis on which our communities can grow into the future.

Despite strong programs for formation, it still remains for congregations to develop consistent expectations of its core leadership with respect to Christian formation.

Despite strong programs for formation, it still remains for congregations to develop consistent expectations of its core leadership with respect to Christian formation. One concrete way forward for a congregation might be to decide (as an example) that as of five years in the future, all holders of congregational offices would be expected to have training and experience in the following four areas:

- A comprehensive introduction to the **scriptures** (commensurate with the DISCIPLE and Covenant Bible study series)

- A comprehensive overview of **Christian doctrines and practices** held and practiced in common between historic Christian communities (commensurate with the Christian Believer series)
- Exposure to the distinct doctrines, practices, and history of **one's own tradition** of Christian formation (i.e., Lutheran, Reformed, Anglican, Baptist, and Methodist traditions of Christian formation)
- A program of intentional Christian **spiritual formation** including accountability for spiritual practices

A congregation that adopts such a protocol would have five years to put in place programs for training and formation along these lines, but many congregations already have components of each of these in place. This might be an area where local congregations could work together across denominational boundaries on all but perhaps the matter of formation in one's own tradition of Christian formation.

Before the end of five years, the congregation would need to be extending its formation and training to build a larger core and to attract new lay leadership for the congregation. Formational activities might be tied to a regular Sunday evening or Wednesday evening period, with a common meal and worship opportunities. A congregation might be able to envision a different way to strengthen its core membership, but strengthening the core membership will be a key to the congregation's growth and vitality into the future.

Engage New Constituencies by Discerning Needs

Once in an idle moment I examined the stained-glass windows in our church in Maryland, looking at the names memorialized and otherwise recorded in them. The amazing fact that struck me, as a student of name origins, was that every single one of the surnames was English. I mean, no Scots names, no Welsh names, no typically Irish names, and certainly nothing beyond the British Isles. All English! Wow. I can't imagine that people with English surnames were the only folks in that community who needed the ministries of that church.

This is a problem for our churches. Despite the fact that the United States has grown *far more ethnically and culturally diverse* since the Immigration and Naturalization Act of 1965, and despite the fact that we are far more *aware* of the varieties of race and culture in the United States today, historic Protestant churches have remained rather solidly tied to their historic ethnic and cultural constituencies:

- German and Scandinavian constituencies for Lutherans
- English-American and Afro-Caribbean-American constituencies for Anglicans including Episcopalians
- British-American and African-American constituencies for Methodists and Baptists
- Scots and Scots-Irish American constituencies for Presbyterians

There is of course an accompanying narrative of origins in each of these cases that accounts for their traditional ethnic and cultural constituencies. But really, if you go out for drinks before dinner at an ecumenical gathering, you can almost predict that the Episcopalians will order sherry, Presbyterians will order scotch, Lutherans will want beer whether they order it or not, and Methodists and Baptists will have iced tea unless there are no other Methodists or Baptists around, in which case they might ask for white zinfandel. We seem almost bound to live out cultural stereotypes and stuck in historic cultural affinity groups of our origins. We've got to break out.

Origins are one thing; our contemporary mission may be otherwise. Might I suggest that this historic predicament is an offense against the catholicity or universality of the church? I do not mean that we should pretend to be people we are not. We have to use the gifts we have been given, and ethnicities and cultures are part of those gifts. But might it be possible, under the leadership of the Holy Spirit, for us to be sensitive to new needs and possibilities that are emerging in our time?

It might make more sense to seek new constituencies based on the needs of a particular community rather than ethnicity or existing denominational ties.

Contemporary efforts to begin new congregations often begin with careful sociological analysis so that marketing messages can be tailored to particular constituencies. They sometimes begin with sociological analysis so that new congregations will not overlap other congregations of a particular Christian tradition. I'm not sure those are good ways to go about the work of seeking new constituencies. It might make more sense to seek new constituencies based on the needs of a particular community rather than ethnicity or existing denominational ties. Sociological analysis can in fact be *very* helpful in this work if we are looking for needs we can meet. But needs we can meet with our own resources might not fit ethnic or linguistic or denominational categories. They might not even fit existing definitions of community boundaries. There's an old saying that "money follows mission," but mission, I would say, should follow needs. A congregation may need to engage in a soul-searching quest for the needs in the world around it that the congregation can address. And it may be that it will take a new congregation to address particular needs.

We may need to ask, for example, if existing church buildings and other structures are what we need for reaching out to new constituencies based on needs. Church buildings institutionalize particular ways of worship, and they may reinforce ethnic and cultural traditions. A pipe organ, a piano, even an electric guitar each presupposes a very specific cultural tradition about worship. Having racks in the back of pews for printed materials or projection screens presuppose something about the way in which worship will be conducted. They may presuppose something about the social class or educational backgrounds of persons attending the congregation. The very fact that we build wooden pews fixed in particular locations (was that ever a good idea?) presupposes a specific tradition of worship. It's sometimes difficult to imagine how alienating these structures may be for people who come from very different cultural traditions. However lovely or comforting they may appear to us, they may be saying to other people, "You are really not welcome here. This is *our* church."

Our existing church structures may be more shackles than resources as we seek new constituencies in the future. For new constituencies, especially if we mean different ethnic and cultural traditions than have characterized our churches in the past, will require us to step outside of culturally defined comfort zones.

Speaking of comfort zones, I'm now well out of my comfort zone as a historian trying to prescribe what present and future practices might be. But I'm also aware of the fact that evangelical as well as historic Protestant communities have had considerable success in attracting new constituencies in recent decades. I suspect that the key lies in being who we are, being clear about our own gifts, and being at the same time open to the movement of the Spirit that makes us sensitive to others. It might help for us to study the ways in which Christians in the past and Christians in the present are relating to new constituencies. Hmmm . . . we might need to listen to missionaries. About our missions in the United States.

Offer Tradition and Continuity as Well as Innovation in Worship Styles

Worship is the area where our openness to other cultural traditions may be most significantly challenged. I have described above the legacies of older Protestant churches in our inherited traditions of worship. Most of us have struggled with issues of balancing these traditions with contemporary expressions especially in music and other forms of artistic presentation accompanying worship. Two matters need to be held in mind:

- On the one hand, there is a core of Christian worship practices that has remained relatively consistent over the centuries. The ecumenical- and liturgical-renewal movements of the twentieth century helped us enormously to recognize just what this core of practices has been, and it helped us grow together as churches as we implemented this nucleus or core of worship practices together.
- On the other hand, this core of practices has little to do with particular styles of music or other means of communicating the gospel in churches. It has little to do with organs, pianos, electric guitars, pews, votive candles, incense, or particular forms of harmony in church music. Even speaking styles and (dare I say it?) lengths of sermons might not be part of the eternally relevant core of Christian worship.

This is not a new set of problems: Isaac Watts and Charles Wesley found it challenging to introduce hymns beyond the metrical psalms that had been sung since the Reformation in Reformed and Anglican churches, and in fact, the use of hymns flourished in informal gatherings (e.g., Methodist societies) long before it was instantiated in Sunday morning services. The same was true with early nineteenth-century spirituals, the Gospel music of the late 1800s and the early 1900s, and more contemporary forms of Gospel and Contemporary Christian music in the twentieth century. All of these musical genres flourished in more informal settings before they became part of more traditional worship. In some contemporary cases, congregations might consider whether an informal gathering with contemporary and culture-specific musical and artistic expressions might be a better option than immediately changing inherited worship styles. It might even provide a workspace for a transition in worship styles.

One of the problems for us is that our conventional prayer books and hymnals have confused together elements of the core of Christian worship with elements of particular cultural traditions: "Here may an hymn or anthem be sung" presupposes a particular form of musical culture. We need to continue a relentlessly honest conversation about what the core of worship is and what amounts to particular cultural expressions of worship. We need to preserve tradition and continuity as regards to the core of worship and allow for innovation and creativity as regards to new cultural expressions of the faith.

We need to continue a relentlessly honest conversation about what the core of worship is and what amounts to particular cultural expressions of worship.

This distinction does not solve all our problems with worship. Just because we choose a certain musical style, for example, does not mean that it will be performed well. And that's another big issue in Christian worship. A lot of congregations experimented with Contemporary Christian worship in the 1990s by asking whoever in the congregation could play a guitar or a drum kit, and they ended up with extraordinarily ~~lousy~~ unsatisfactory instances of that genre. That is to say, if a congregation moves from traditional classical music to Contemporary Christian music or Christian folk music or mariachi masses or Afro-Caribbean styles of Christian music, the congregation still has to worry about expertise in musical leadership and performance, and the overhead (instruments, amplification, performance equipment, projection screens, books, copyrights and performance rights, and so on) that particular musical or performance styles require.

Marketing

We've got to think seriously about marketing. Yes, I know "marketing" sounds as though we do a survey of what people want and then deliver some form of cool religion as a customer-designed product to suit their own personal needs, disregarding the scriptures and tradition and uncomfortable stuff like that. No doubt we could sell eight commandments a lot easier than ten, especially if we allowed people to choose which two commandments they want to dis from month to month. Wouldn't that be ~~cool?~~ ~~interesting?~~ ~~fun?~~ immoral? But marketing doesn't have to be quite that sinister. The only alternative I can envision is to continue to let others define our identities instead of defining them for ourselves.

One of the most critical reasons for churches taking up marketing strategies is that our churches are in fact the *objects* of marketing strategies. I don't just mean the generic marketing that bombards all of us hourly urging us to purchase cars and jewelry and food and drinks. I mean the marketing that is specifically directed at Protestant Christian communities pressing them to use mass-marketed versions of Christian literature and licenses to use mass-marketed versions of Christian music.

One of the most critical reasons for churches taking up marketing strategies is that our churches are in fact the* objects *of marketing strategies.

Do sophisticated literature- and music-marketing corporations function as a New Vatican, decreeing by their massively successful marketing strategies what words Christians will sing, what prayers they will pray, and how they will worship? Bottom line: they are not responsible to churches, certainly not to historic Protestant churches. The problem is not, as indicated above, with any particular genre or cultural expression of music. It has been a great strength of our churches to adopt (sometimes cautiously) new musical and cultural styles of worship. The problem is more often that musical genres are often packaged and marketed together with very particular forms of worship that do not have a place for the liturgical traditions and liturgical consensus that have also been strengths of our churches. But again, if our churches do not employ their own marketing strategies, we will consistently fall prey to the marketing choices of others.

Marketing does not have to mean selling products to external constituencies. Author Steven Levy points out that the Apple marketing campaign "Think Different" in the late 1990s was not only aimed at attracting people to buy Apple computers. It attempted to change the internal culture of Apple after Steve Jobs returned to the company in 1996. The era at Apple ushered in by the "Think Different" campaign had some stunning, creative results, like iMacs, iPods, iPhones, and iPads. The unleashing of this creativity contributed to building Apple into one of the strongest companies in the world within a few years. So marketing does not simply involve representing ourselves to external constituencies; it can involve changing our perceptions of ourselves. What's been said earlier in this book makes a strong case that we need to change some of our faulty perceptions of ourselves before we are able to represent ourselves better to people outside the boundaries of church cultures.

I want to make a case for professionalism as churches engage marketing. Marketing has become an extraordinarily complex field in recent decades, and it calls for knowledge of a huge variety of contemporary media, how media are used, and how the results of these uses of media are studied and interpreted. Both of our daughters work in the area of social media marketing. They do not spend their days tweeting and taking pics, as one might imagine. They spend a lot of time with data streams aggregated into spreadsheets, learning who's viewing what media, when, and how that might be utilized in fund-raising and other activities. Marketing requires contemporary expertise.

But at the heart of marketing should be the ancient wisdom that says, "know yourself." Marketing is sinister when it attempts to steer groups of people into being something other than who they are, and especially when it attempts to steer people into buying products they don't need or, to put it in terms closer to Christian congregations, to convince us to put our energies into phantom needs rather than the real needs of our communities. Marketing can be effective when it helps groups meet real needs, but not with artificial solutions. Rather, marketing helps when it enables groups to address real needs with the distinctive resources their groups already possess. Like the gospel. And the gospel is not copyrighted.

Gaining Confidence by Speaking on Behalf of Communities

We gain strength and confidence from our communities, but I'm convinced that we need to learn or relearn the habit of speaking on behalf of communities. When I hear homilies at Catholic churches, I tend to hear relentless discussions of the teachings of the Catholic Church. When I hear sermons at Methodist or Reformed or Baptist churches, by contrast, I hear relentless discussions of the pastor's own personal opinions about the scriptures and contemporary issues as if nothing had interposed between the scriptures and the present time and as if their communities of faith had nothing to say. Perhaps Anglican and Lutheran congregations do a better job of this than Methodists, Reformed folks, or Baptists. But all of us need to speak on behalf of communities in order to edify or build up our communities and to give us the confidence that comes of standing within a community of belief. By "communities," I mean not only local congregations but our traditions of Christian formation as well, that is, our traditions as Anglicans, Lutherans, Baptists, Disciples, and Reformed folks.

Speaking on behalf of communities does not mean lockstep declaration of the teachings of churches. It means speaking accurately about the consensus that churches have developed as churches or as communities about Christian teachings and practices. It must engage critical contemporary reflection on those teachings and practices. It should also involve speaking about ecumenical consensus where our denominational traditions have come to agreement about specific Christian teachings and practices.

Speaking on behalf of communities does not mean lockstep declaration of the teachings of churches. It means speaking accurately about the consensus that churches have developed as churches or as communities about Christian teachings and practices.

Knowing what we have agreed to teach and practice together builds confidence in communities. I would hope for a rich balance of reflection on the Christian scriptures, Christian traditions, contemporary ecumenical agreements, the teachings of our own denominational or confessional traditions, agreements within a local community, as well as our own critical, contemporary reflections on these teachings and practices. Perhaps that's asking a lot of Christian leaders, but most Christian leaders trained in theological schools have been exposed to critical study of the scriptures, critical study of the Christian tradition, and the study of their own church or denominational traditions. I'm suggesting that sermons and other forms of teaching in our churches should reflect these areas of knowledge of church culture as a way of building up our communities. Ecumenical consensus is not taught as consistently at theological schools, so this may be an area where we need to offer special help for Christian leaders today.

It's really important to distinguish *what churches profess together* as communities in contrast to the opinions that individual church members or even church leaders may express. Just because Marietta, who belongs to a Presbyterian church, thinks that only believers should be baptized, doesn't mean that the Presbyterian Church (U.S.A.) believes that only believers should be baptized. They don't. Just because John who is an Episcopal bishop expresses doubts about traditional beliefs about Jesus doesn't mean that the Episcopal Church in the USA shares his doubts about traditional beliefs about Jesus. They don't, not as a community of people.

But whether they acknowledge it or not, there's a crucial distinction between individuals' personal beliefs and the beliefs professed by their churches as formal bodies. I'm convinced that we gain confidence by knowing the beliefs professed by our churches as communities, and it's utterly important to distinguish our churches' professed beliefs from the opinions of church members or church leaders or even individual theologians.

Church teachings are not a matter of Gallup polls of church members. Churches define their own teachings through their processes for coming to agreement. That means that the General Assembly of the Presbyterian Church (U.S.A.) enunciates the formal teachings and the authorized forms of worship of the PC(USA). The General Convention of the Episcopal Church determines the formal teachings and the authorized worship practices of that body of Christians.

Don't be charmed into thinking that theologians speak on behalf of communities of Christians. Many theologians consider it their professional responsibility to challenge the teachings of their churches. They very often understand their roles not as defenders of the faith but as prophetic challengers of received or traditional teachings and practices. They often presuppose that people have already been formed or catechized in traditional teachings. That presupposition doesn't always work these days, as any of us in theological schools can tell you. Sometimes we have formed students who know more about contemporary critiques of traditional teachings than they do about the traditional teachings and practices they suppose themselves to be critiquing. That's a genuine problem.

It's also a genuine problem when clergy and other church leaders don't distinguish their own opinions from the teachings of their churches. It's even worse when clergy deliver only their own opinions and do not speak or act on behalf of their churches. Most of our churches require clergy to pledge that they will speak on behalf of their church and will represent its teachings fairly. In my denomination, The United Methodist Church, we ask candidates for the ordained ministry of elders to promise in the presence of witnesses that they will "preach and maintain our doctrines." This doesn't exclude them from expressing their own opinions. It does require them to speak on behalf of the church and its communally defined beliefs. Speaking on behalf of a community of faith builds confidence within that community.

Rethinking Denominations and Ways of Being Christian

But this raises the critical issue of whether we're asked to speak on behalf of specific denominations as institutions or as they represent distinctive traditions of Christian faith. One of the reasons why pastors and other Christian leaders may be reluctant to speak on behalf of communities today is because naming specific denominations can sound like we're just advocating a kind of mindless institutional loyalty. Perhaps this is not as important an item as the previous ones, but we need a different way of thinking about why it really is important to talk about being Methodist, Presbyterian, Anglican, Reformed, or Lutheran.

The marketing value of denominational names seems to have fallen significantly in recent decades, and not just in historic churches. A Dallas-area megachurch officially called "Prestonwood Baptist Church" now brands itself as "Prestonwood Church" in much of its signage and marketing. The truth is that most of us with ecumenical sensibilities are really not out to advocate one denomination over others, at least, not as an institution.

Denominational traditions are ways of being Christian that can't be ignored.

But denominational traditions are ways of being Christian that can't be ignored. There is an Anglican way of being Christian, whether you're part of the Episcopal Church in the USA or any of the other forms of Anglicanism throughout the world. If The United Methodist Church divides into the Open Methodist Church and the Orthodox Methodist Church and the Church of Ted (my own designer denomination), we will all continue to share a sense of being part of a Wesleyan and Methodist way of being Christian.

The well-concealed truth is that contemporary megachurches with no overt denominational affiliations do in fact represent particular ways of being Christian parallel to historic denominational traditions. The Willow Creek Community Church in South Barrington, Illinois, has roots in the Evangelical Free Church of America, a denomination that grew from Scandinavian Pietist and evangelical movements among immigrants to North America. Although it is not connected directly to the denomination and does not advertise its roots in that denomination, it does in fact share in this particular way of being Christian. The Saddleback Church of Lake Forest, California, has roots in the Southern Baptist way of being Christian. The Southeast Christian Church of Louisville, Kentucky, has roots in the traditions of Disciples of Christ and Churches of Christ. While denominational names may have disappeared from church signs and even from institutional affiliations, denominational ways of being Christian are alive and well today.

Boring as they may be, denominations *even as institutions* are probably necessary. For example, they carry out work like vetting candidates for ministry, the coordination of ministries, and negotiating ecumenical alliances. But if the institutions themselves aren't contributing to confidence in our churches, understanding ourselves as inheritors of particular ways of being Christian *can* contribute to confidence on the part of contemporary Christian communities.

A program of Christian formation needs to include formation in the history, the teachings, and the distinctive practices of particular ways of being Christian.

A program of Christian formation needs to include formation in *the history, the teachings, and the distinctive practices of particular ways of being Christian.* This can't be dismissed as merely institutional work and it can't be taught as merely structural or institutional elements of a church's organization. Christians need to understand the particular ways in which they have been formed. And we can learn our own ways of being Christian in dialogue with other ways of being Christian without calling into question the integrity of other ways. Learning our own traditions in dialogue with others points us again to what we believe and practice in common, and that builds confidence in Christian communities.

Grace

> Look to the rock from which you were cut,
> and to the quarry from where you were dug.
> Look to Abraham your ancestor,
> and to Sarah, who gave you birth. (Isa 51:1-2).

It's worthwhile to expose some of the more pernicious myths about our churches, especially for folks in our churches. We're less likely to convince anyone outside. It's worth stating some of the facts about our present situation, assessing our legacies and our strengths, and considering ways forward. But we do not move forward by ourselves.

We look to our roots for renewal. Christian communities have tried the experiment of jettisoning the past and lurching forward without foundations. The results were sometimes spectacular, and sometimes spectacularly short-lived. As a tree grows, its roots need to spread deeper and wider. We do not move forward without a foundation. Strengthen the core. Tend to the roots. "Look to the rock from which you were cut" (Isa 51:1).

In the end we want to say that the rock is Christ. We want to say that our communities are "built on the foundation of the apostles and prophets with Christ Jesus himself as the cornerstone" (Eph 2:20).

And in the end we want to say that the rock is Christ (1 Cor 10:4). We want to say that our communities are "built on the foundation of the apostles and prophets with Christ Jesus himself as the cornerstone" (Eph 2:20). If our buildings are wasted and our pension funds dry up and our church resolutions fall on deaf ears and our collection plates go empty, we will continue to proclaim "Jesus Christ, and to preach him as crucified" (1 Cor 2:2), through the water of baptism by which we are buried and raised with him, through bread and wine by which we celebrate Christ's presence and "proclaim [his] death until he comes" (1 Cor 11:26 NRSV).

In the end, there's not much more to say. The preservation of the church, the renewal of the church is not our work. It's God's work. It's grace. And that's good news. *beep* *beep* *beep* *beep*

NOTES

Foreword

Bishop Kevin Kanouse's foreword refers to Robert Bacher and Kenneth Inskeep, *Chasing Down a Rumor: The Death of the Mainline Denominations* (Minneapolis: Augsburg Fortress, 2005).

1. Myths

Dean M. Kelley's *Why Conservative Churches Are Growing: A Study in Sociology of Religion* was originally published by Random House (New York, 1972). A revised edition with an updated preface was published by Mercer University Press (Macon, GA) in 1986.

Martin Marty recounted ABC's firing of Peggy Wehmeyer in his *Sightings* column for July 16, 2001, "More News of Religion News" (https://divinity.uchicago.edu/sightings/more-news-religion-news). Marty noted in that column that ABC had cited fiscal reasons for the firing, but Wehmeyer herself gave an account of her firing in a public address on January 22, 2002, at Garrett-Evangelical Theological Seminary in which she described dismissive attitudes of news executives (not just at ABC) as the underlying grounds for her dismissal.

With the confirmation of Elena Kagan as a US Supreme Court justice in August 2010, the court no longer had any self-identified Protestants; see "Supreme Court Likely to Have No Protestants," *Christian Century* 127, no. 12 (June 15, 2010), 16–17.

Various reports that the US no longer had a majority of citizens identifying themselves as Protestants were circulated from as early as 2004, but by 2012 the fact was widely reported based on Pew Research findings released that year; see "US Protestants No Longer a Majority - study," BBC News, October 10, 2012, http://www.bbc.com/news/world-us-canada-19892837.

Jon Stewart made the comment about Methodists during an episode of *The Daily Show*. Jon Stewart, "Wedding of the Decade of the Century of the Millennium," *The Daily Show* video, 5:53, August 2, 2010, http://thedaily show.cc.com/videos/mjj09s/wedding-of-the-decade-of-the-century-of-the -millennium.

The quotation from US Rep. Rick Santorum, including the audio recording of the speech, was reported by Ryan Grim in "Rick Santorum In 2008: Mainstream Protestantism Fell Out Of 'World Of Christianity,'" *Huffington Post*, February 18, 2012, http://www.huffingtonpost .com/2012/02/18/rick-santorum-protestantism_n_1286471.html.

The quotation from Joseph Bottum is from his article "The Death of Protestant America: A Political Theory of the Protestant Mainline," *First Things* 185 (August–September 2008): 30.

The list of denominations I consider to be "historic Protestant" or "mainline" or "old-line" is very similar to that given in the Bacher and Inskeep work cited above in Bishop Kevin Kanouse's foreword, cf. 39 and 49–57. I have broadened the definition somewhat by including some historically black denominations (AME, AME Zion, and CME) and by including the more recently organized Cooperative Baptist Fellowship.

2. Facts

Much of the material in this chapter is adapted from my article "Glory Days? The Myth of the Mainline," in *Christian Century* 131, no. 14 (July 9, 2014). Used by permission.

Martin Marty wrote about "MainlineDecline, Decline-Talk, and Decline-ism" in his *Sightings* column for July 22, 2013, https://divinity.uchicago .edu/sightings/mainlinedecline-decline-talk-and-decline-ism-martin-e -marty.

Bacher and Inskeep also present a series of statistics in their chapter on "Numbers" (*Chasing Down a Rumor*, 83–109), though their statistics are oriented toward illustrating the extent to which denominational loyalty and group meanings are still functioning today.

Membership figures for US mainline denominations and their predecessors for 1925, 1950, 1975, and 2000 are given as they appear in the Association of Religion Data Archives (thearda.com) under "Religious Groups," then under "Religious Group Profiles." Some cautions about the use of these figures are given in the text. US population figures are given from federal census figures, though the 1925 and 1975 figures are interpolated from 1920 and 1930 and from 1970 and 1980, respectively.

Changes in US religious life resulting from the Immigration and Nationality Act of 1965 are documented in Diana L. Eck, *A New Religious America* (San Francisco: HarperCollins, 2001).

The decline in percentages for persons describing themselves as evangelical or "born again" Christians in the United States from 21 percent in 2007 to 19 percent in 2012 is reported in a Pew Center study in its "Religion and Public Life" series, dated October 9, 2012; see www.pewforum.org/2012/10/09/nones-on-the-rise/. The latest Pew Religious Landscape report (May 2015) confirms the trend that secularization is affecting all US religious communities.

Weekly average attendance figures for the Episcopal Church in the USA, the Evangelical Lutheran Church in America, the Presbyterian Church (U.S.A), and The United Methodist Church (in the United States figures only) are given in the *Episcopal Church Annual* (the "Red Book"); the figure for 1990 attendance is actually 1991, the first year of reporting; figures supplied by the division of Research and Evaluation of the ELCA; figures supplied by the Office of Research Services of the PC(USA); and summaries of figures at the beginning of The United Methodist Church *General Minutes* (online versions in more recent years).

The discovery that weekly religious attendance in the United States is closer to 21 percent than the consistently self-reported figure of 40 percent is documented in two articles: C. Kirk Hadaway, Penny Long Marler, and Mark Chaves, "What the Polls Don't Show: A Closer Look at U.S. Church Attendance," *American Sociological Review* 58, no. 6 (December 1993): 741–52; and C. Kirk Hadaway and Penny Long Marler, "How Many Americans Attend Worship Each Week? An Alternative Approach to Measurement," *Journal for the Scientific Study of Religion* 44, no. 3 (2005): 307–22.

Mark Chaves shows that there has not been a large-scale exodus from historic Protestant churches to evangelical churches in *American Religion: Contemporary Trends* (Princeton, NJ: Princeton University Press, 2011), 81–93.

3. Legacies

The legacy of postmillennial optimism and social activism grounded in this outlook in US Protestant churches has been documented by James H. Moorhead in *World Without End: Mainstream American Protestant Visions of the Last Things, 1880–1925* (Bloomington: Indiana University Press, 1999). The rise of premillennialism is documented by George M. Marsden in *Fundamentalism and American Culture* (New York: Oxford University Pres

1980).

The notion of the "two-party system" in American Protestantism from the 1890s forward was suggested by Martin E. Marty in *The Righteous Empire: The Protestant Experience in America* (New York: Dial Press, 1970).

The work of Lucy Rider Meyer in Chicago is described by her biographer Isabelle Horton in *High Adventure: The Life of Lucy Rider Meyer* (New York and Cincinnati: Methodist Book Concern, 1928).

A comprehensive study of the phenomena of evangelical revival and awakening movements in the United States is that of William G. McLoughlin, *Revivals, Awakenings, and Reform*, Chicago History of American Religion, ed. Martin E. Marty (Chicago: University of Chicago Press, 1978). A prominent study of the Second Great Awakening is that of Nathan Hatch, *The Democratization of American Religion* (New Haven, CT: Yale University Press, 1989).

The parallel movements I have described as representing "high-church" and confessional forms of conservatism in the 1800s are described by Walter H. Conser Jr., in *Church and Confession: Conservative Theologians in Germany, England, and America, 1815–1866* (Macon, GA: Mercer University Press, 1984).

Henry McNeal Turner made his case for the "presbyteral" succession of Methodist clergy in *The Genius and Theory of Methodist Polity: Or, The Machinery of Methodism* (1885; repr., Nashville: AMEC Sunday School Union, 1986), ch. 2. He was also influential in getting the AME Church to adopt John Wesley's form of *The Book of Common Prayer* (*The Sunday Service of the Methodists in North America*, originally published in 1784) as the authorized liturgy of the AME Church.

Thesis 62 of Luther's *Ninety-Five Theses on the Power and Efficacy of Indulgences* (1517) is translated from the text that appears in *D. Martin Luthers Werke: Kritische Gesamtausgabe* (Weimar: Hermann Böhlaus Nachfolger, 1926), 1:236. The translation is my own.

The sentence "God is nice and we ought to be nice too" sounds like something I've heard Stanley Hauerwas say. Not approvingly.

Excerpts from the Apostles' Creed and the Nicene Creed are cited from *The United Methodist Hymnal* (Nashville: The United Methodist Publishing House, 1989), 880–82.

The acclamations in the service for the Lord's Supper are given as they appear in "Word and Table I, II, and III," in *The United Methodist Hymnal*, 10, 14, and 16.

4. Strengths

The "Brief Statement of Faith" inherited from the Presbyterian Church (U.S.A) is given in *The Constitution of the Presbyterian Church (U.S.A), Part I: Book of Confessions* (Louisville: Office of the General Assembly, 2007), 267–68. The contemporary "Declaratory Statement" on the teaching about predestination from the PC(USA) is cited from the same publication, 163–64.

Excerpts from *The Book of Common Prayer* are cited from Brian Cummings, ed., *The Book of Common Prayer: The Texts of 1549, 1559, and 1662* (Oxford: Oxford University Press, 2011), from the 1662 service, 434 and 399.

Questions for persons presenting themselves for membership in The United Methodist Church are cited from *The United Methodist Hymnal*, 34–35.

The quotation from Neal Town Stephenson's *Cryptonomicon* (New York: Avon Books, 1999) about small denominational colleges appears on p. 50.

5. Future

An "Afterword to the Revised Edition" of Steven Levy's *Insanely Great: The Life and Times of Macintosh, the Computer That Changed Everything*, 2nd ed. (New York: Penguin Books, 2000) describes the "Think Different" campaign: "But the campaign was directed as much to excite the people inside Apple as its potential customers. As Jobs explained, the message was, 'This is who we are, guys—If you don't want to be this, get off the bus'" (p. 361).

The expression "Know Yourself" was given by the Greek geographer Pausanias as an inscription at the temple of Apollo at Delphi in W. H. S. Jones, tr., *Pausanias: Description of Greece*, vol. 4, Loeb Classical Library (Cambridge, MA: Harvard University Press, 1956), 506–7.

Bacher and Inskeep make a similar distinction to what I'm describing as "institutional" attachment to denominations and the broader category of contemporary "ways of being Christian." Throughout the book, they stress the importance of building cultures that can be transmitted trans-generationally; see the conclusion of ch. 5, "Built to Last" (*Chasing Down a Rumor*, 117–20).